"A Very Fine Class of Immigrants"

PRINCE EDWARD ISLAND'S SCOTTISH PIONEERS

1770–1850

"A Very Fine Class of Immigrants"

PRINCE EDWARD ISLAND'S SCOTTISH PIONEERS
1770–1850

LUCILLE H. CAMPEY

NATURAL HERITAGE BOOKS
TORONTO

Published by Natural Heritage/Natural History Inc.
P.O. Box 95, Station O, Toronto, Ontario M4A 2M8

Cover illustration: Charlottetown from Thompson's Hill,
by George Hubbard, 1844, *courtesy of Prince Edward Island
Museum and Heritage Foundation, HF.74.12.1.*
Back cover illustration: Charlotte Harbour by George Thresher,
c. 1830, *courtesy of Prince Edward Island
Public Archives and Records Office, Acc. 2916/1.*

Edited by Jane Gibson.
Design by Blanche Hamill, Norton Hamill Design

Printed and bound in Canada by Hignell Printing Limited

Canadian Cataloguing in Publication Data

Campey, Lucille H.
A very fine class of immigrants :
Prince Edward Island's Scottish pioneers, 1770–1850

Includes bibliographical references and index.
ISBN 1-896219-10-1

1. Scots-Prince Edward Island–History. 2. Scotland–Emigration and immigration-
History. 3. Prince Edward Island–Emigration and immigration--History. I. Title.

FC2650.S3C35 2001   304.8'7170411   C2001-930556-7
F1049.7.S4C35 2001

THE CANADA COUNCIL | LE CONSEIL DES ARTS
FOR THE ARTS | DU CANADA
SINCE 1957 | DEPUIS 1957

We acknowledge the financial support of the Government of Canada through
the Book Publishing Industry Development Program (BPIDP) for our publishing
activities, the support received for our publishing program from the Canada
Council Block Grant Program and the assistance of the Association for the
Export of Canadian Books, Ottawa.

To Geoff

CONTENTS

TABLES AND FIGURES

TABLES

FIGURES

PREFACE

SCOTS WHO OPTED for pioneer life in Prince Edward Island form the subject of this book. Being the first of the so-called northern colonies to be sold off in its entirety to proprietors, in the late eighteenth century, the Island acquired its Scots earliest, doing so even before the start of the American War of Independence in 1775. Prince Edward Island's colonisation by Scots, thus, takes us back to a period when the process of emigration and settlement formation were in their infancy.

I first visited the Public Archives and Records Office in Charlottetown when I was in the data gathering stages of my doctoral thesis. Having completed my work earlier than expected, I had just enough free time to drive to Belfast, which lies to the southeast of Charlottetown. I had no real academic justification for the visit but felt, for some inexplicable reason, that it would produce something useful.

As I approached Belfast, the researcher in me eyed the Presbyterian church and nearby cemetery very critically and duly noted down the questions which I would ponder upon my returned home to Scotland. It was only when I walked up to Lord Selkirk's memorial that I began properly to take in my surroundings. Some 800 Highlanders and Islanders had come in 1803 under Selkirk's watchful eye, and with his financial backing, to colonise the Belfast area. As I looked up and from to side to side, I felt an overwhelming sense of awe. It dawned on me, there and then for the first time, that I was actually looking at a landscape which had been cleared by the very people who had come out from Scotland with Selkirk. They were some of the Island's early pioneers who had hacked their way through miles of bush and wilderness. They were amongst the ones commemorated in the neat rows of tombstones which stretched out before me. There was a strong sense of Scottishness in the place, as inscription after inscription proudly recorded that this or that person "was a native of Skye" or some other region of Scotland.

Looking back, it is hardly surprising that this place made such a marked impression on me. My dissertation was concerned with the regional aspects of Scottish emigration to Canada. I was establishing the areas of Scotland from which emigrants had originated, then trying to find their new locations in Canada, and in this case, on the Island. There, in the Belfast cemetery, tombstones were telling me of Scottish regional origins. Because the Island's Genealogical Society had published tombstone inscriptions for this and other cemeteries on the Island, I was able to take this geographical data home with me to study and correlate with other sources. Through their publication, which includes newspaper death notices, I established the geographical origins and settlement locations on the Island for over 750 Scots. Having done so, I could then move on to question the significance of their settlement choices.

In pursuing this line of research, I was essentially identifying factors which may have attracted Scots to the Island. Some may find this approach provocative and contentious, believing all emigration to be the result of forced departures and extreme destitution. Much of the surviving documentary evidence and previous research on emigration has in fact been preoccupied with the pressures on the poor and dispossessed to leave the Highlands and Islands of Scotland. However, this is not to say that emigration from Scotland was concentrated in just one region or around the very poor. It was not. Emigration was a country-wide movement of people of differing means who were influenced by many factors. And one of the crucial factors which influenced them was the prospect of a better and more economically advantageous life abroad.

The key to this better life was timber. For a number of reasons, Scots, more so than the Irish or English, were drawn first to the timber-producing regions of the eastern Maritimes. In fact, the Scots who came to Prince Edward Island during the late eighteenth and early nineteenth centuries were some of the earliest settlers to exploit the benefits to be had from the regions' rapidly expanding timber trade with Britain. I wondered why the early exodus from Scotland to the Island was principally from the west side of Scotland. I also wondered why was it that sustained emigration from Dumfriesshire began so much later than was the case elsewhere in Scotland. To answer these questions I needed to understand Scotland's trade and shipping links with the Island and thanks to my husband's familiarity with the world of shipping, I soon became acquainted with something called *Lloyd's List.*

It seemed to me incredible that a documentary source, which is still in use today, could reveal the ports of arrival and departure of the ships which took emigrants from Scotland to the Island over 200 years ago. Knowledge of the safe arrival of ships and reliable shipping intelligence, provided through *Lloyd's List,* has long been the mainstay of insurers, merchants and ship owners. Through the use of paid correspondents at the main ports, detailed records were kept and published from the late eighteenth century, and it was this data which enabled me to reconstruct the two-way journeys taken by emigrant ships. Obtaining cargo information from the Scottish customs records, I could see a clear pattern. After leaving their home ports, ships stopped at Highland and Island ports such as Oban, Tobermory and Stornoway to collect emigrants before heading west across the Atlantic to Charlottetown. They returned immediately back to Scotland with a timber load. Here was evidence of a two-way traffic in people and timber as shippers capitalised on the enthusiasm in the Highlands and Islands for emigration and the availability of wilderness land in Prince Edward Island. Crucial to the process was the accessibility of sea transport. It favoured potential emigrants who lived near ports which had early trade links with the Island or who could be conveniently collected by passing timber ships.

My second foray into shipping sources came when I discovered the *Lloyd's Shipping Register*. Still in use today, it remains the authoritative source on a ship's age, condition and quality of construction. Merchants and insurers risked their money on its reliability and accuracy and we therefore have to give it high credibility as a source. The Register might have been consulted back in 1803 by Lord Selkirk's agents when they advised on ships to take the Skye and Uist emigrants to Belfast. It was probably not just a coincidence that of the three ships which sailed to the Island, the only one to have a top "A1" rating was the ship that Lord Selkirk, himself, had sailed on. However, the other two ships were perfectly seaworthy, as were most of the ships which were used to carry emigrants from Scotland to the Island. Before my acquaintance with the *Lloyd's Shipping Register*, I would have assumed that there was some basis for the popular view that all emigrants had miserable crossings in substandard and battered ships. The Register is a salutary reminder that anecdotal meanderings are a poor substitute for hard facts. From it we must conclude that, although ludicrously inadequate by modern day standards, most of the ships which took Scottish emigrants to Prince Edward Island were among the best or nearly best available of their time.

A lasting memory of my visit to Belfast cemetery was the feeling that I had stumbled into a place which still cherishes its Scottish roots. One of the constant themes which I found myself returning to was the importance of strong family and community ties in cementing early settlements and in sustaining follow-on emigration from the areas of Scotland which had fostered the original footholds. The uncompromising resolve of Scottish groups to exclude outside influences and to perpetuate their own customs gave their communities a distinctive collective identity. Lord Selkirk had understood this when he insisted that religious divides and spaces for extended families to follow should be delineated right from the beginning at Belfast. Even before this, in the 1790s, Father MacEachern had directed Scottish Roman Catholics to separate areas on the Island which were within his reach and care. The

Dumfriesshire-born Walter Johnstone also recognised the huge importance that religious observance played in early pioneer communities, and was instrumental in establishing Sabbath Schools and in furthering Presbyterian worship on the Island. And Andrew MacDonald, in his own way, represents another strand in Scottish clannishness. I had first noticed him in the Scottish customs records of 1806. What a sight he must have made on his arrival with 36 camp ovens, 48 frying pans and a large assortment of household equipment and tools. Less visible would have been the capital he brought with him and his head for business, since in no time at all he established himself as a successful storekeeper. Such men were pivotal in pioneer communities and it is highly likely that his business interests would have excluded all but fellow Scots.

We might sympathise with the Island's pioneer Scots who had to leave their country behind, but they should also command our respect. They showed tremendous courage and determination, and most were successful. Nationalism does not always bring out the best in people but on the Island it was a powerful force for good, and its strength still rings loud and clear from many of its gravestones.

ACKNOWLEDGEMENTS

THERE ARE MANY people who encouraged and helped me in the research and writing of this book. I am particularly indebted to Dr. Marjory Harper, of Aberdeen University, who supervised my dissertation and continues to be a source of advice, help and encouragement. A special thank you goes to Marilyn Bell of the Prince Edward Island Public Archives and Record Office for suggesting that I read *From Scotland to Prince Edward Island*, the genealogical source which proved so invaluable to me. I am grateful to Rosemary Bigwood for directing me to the Collectors Quarterly Accounts and Court of Sessions Productions at the Scottish Record Office and to staff at the National Library of Scotland who brought several key manuscript sources to my attention. I am also grateful for the unstinting help given to me by staff at Aberdeen University, both from the main Queen Mother Library and the Manuscripts and Special Collections Department. I am also indebted to staff at the Public Record Office and British Library. Finally, I owe a special thank you to Bob Steward of the Highland Council Archives and to the staff at the Inverness Library for their help during my many visits there.

As well, I am very grateful to many people for their help in obtaining the illustrations used in this book. In particular my thanks goes out to Boyde Beck, Curator of History at the Prince Edward Island Museum and Heritage Foundation. His knowledge of what was available and where to find it was invaluable to me as was his assistance in obtaining illustrations from the Meacham's 1880 Atlas. I am also indebted to Dr. Edward MacDonald, Director of Research at the Institute of Island Studies at the University of Prince Edward Island for his general advice and for pointing out illustrative material that I would otherwise not have discovered. I am grateful to David Forsyth, Research Assistant at the National Museums of Scotland for taking so much trouble to help me identify possible illustrations and for his interest in my book. I thank Charlotte Stewart, Research Assistant at the Public Archives and Records Office of Prince Edward Island for her patience and expert friendly guidance and I also owe a special thanks to Mrs. Marjorie MacLauchlan, Director of the Stanhope Historical Society for allowing me to use her Society's photograph of the cairn commemorating the arrival of Scottish settlers on the *Falmouth* in 1770.

I would also like to acknowledge the part played by my own family roots. My great-great-grandfather, William Thomson, left Drainie (Lossiemouth area) in Morayshire in the early 1800s and, but for a last minute change, would have settled in Prince Edward Island. Instead he and his family went to Digby, Nova Scotia, and later to Antigonish where he established a farm at West River. I mention him because my search for him in Scotland and Nova Scotia inspired my interest in early Scottish emigration and greatly influenced my approach to the subject.

There are also a great many others who have helped me in the writing of this book. In particular I would like to thank Miss Jean Lucas who read the first draft and provided many helpful comments and criticisms. But, my greatest debt is to my husband Geoff, without whom this book would not have been possible. Sharing my enthusiasm for the subject, he has given unwavering support and help over the years in so many ways. I have reason to be grateful that he has first-hand knowledge of international shipping, for his computer skills and for his never-failing willingness to discuss emigration matters. This book is dedicated, with love, to him.

ABBREVIATIONS

AH	*Aberdeen Herald*
CB	*Dictionary of Canadian Biography*
DGC	*Dumfries and Galloway Courier and Herald*
DWJ	*Dumfries Weekly Journal*
GC	*Glasgow Courier*
GH	*Glasgow Herald*
GA	*Greenock Advertiser*
IC	*Inverness Courier*
IJ	*Inverness Journal*
IM	*Island Magazine*
NAC	National Archives of Canada
NLS	National Library of Scotland
PANB	Public Archives of New Brunswick
PANS	Public Archives of Nova Scotia
PAPEI	Public Archives of Prince Edward Island
PEIG	*Prince Edward Island Gazette*
PEI Gen. Soc.	Prince Edward Island Genealogical Society
PEIRG	*Prince Edward Island Royal Gazette*
PP	Parliamentary Papers
PRO	Public Record Office
QG	*Quebec Gazette*
QM	*Quebec Mercury*
SCA	Scottish Catholic Archives
SG	*Scottish Genealogist*
SM	*Scots Magazine*
SRO	Scottish Record Office

"It is with singular pleasure we announce the arrival of those honest and worthy Caledonian emigrants, (whom we before mentioned to have embarked for this Island) in health and spirits, notwithstanding a very tedious passage of many weeks. There is not a doubt but that they will receive a kind reception, and experience that hospitality which so characteristically and eminently distinguishes the Highland race."

Royal Gazette and Miscellany of
the Island of St. John, (P.E.I.),
29 July 1791

"A Very Fine Class of Immigrants"

Prince Edward Island's Scottish Pioneers
1770–1850

I

PUSH, PULL AND OPPORTUNITY

"Isabella Howat, wife of James Gregor, died Feb. 29, 1844 in the
76th year of her age. She emigrated from Scotland to this Island
in 1775 and shared all the privations of the early settlers."[1]

A GREAT MANY Scots left their native land in the late eighteenth and
early nineteenth centuries to chance their luck in the wilds of Prince
Edward Island. This movement of people was not simply a flight from
poverty, or the result of expulsions by rapacious landlords, as is generally believed. The factors which pulled Scots to the Island were in
fact every bit as important as those which made them want to leave.
Some of the earliest and most enduring Scottish settlements are to be
found at Belfast, located just to the southeast of Charlottetown. Even
today the place leaves us in no doubt of the importance of its Scottish
roots. A visit to its cemetery speaks volumes, not just of the geographical origins of early Scots, but of the importance placed on
shared ethnic origins. Here, row after row of tombstones tells us of
the people from Skye and other parts of the northwest Highlands and
Islands who wish us to know of their Scottish past. For many, the simple caption, "emigrated in the ship *Polly* to this Island in 1803," tells
its own story. As we view this evocative scene and read the inscriptions, we wonder why so many were drawn to Belfast from this one
part of Scotland.

Thomas Douglas Selkirk, the fifth Earl of Selkirk (1771–1820), *courtesy of P.E.I. Public Archives and Records office, Charlottetown Camera Club Collection, Acc. 2320/3–13.*

The nearby memorial commemorating Thomas Douglas Selkirk, the fifth Earl of Selkirk, reminds us of the pivotal role of this one man in launching the Belfast settlements. Having acquired vast acreages in Prince Edward Island in the early 1800s, and needing to find willing settlers, he cast his net in those parts of Scotland which at the time were showing the greatest interest in emigration. It was in the Western Isles, west Invernessshire and Wester Ross where, because of the dramatic changes taking place at the time in agricultural production, there was a swift response to Selkirk's emigration venture. The introduction from the late eighteenth century of commercially based farming methods and agricultural improvements had resulted in extensive population movements in these areas and the economic prospects for many were bleak. Against this background, the prospect of becoming a landowner in North America and having far better long term economic prospects and security seemed irresistible to people with a sense of adventure and enterprise as well as sufficient capital to finance their journeys.

Lord Selkirk actively encouraged this rising tide of interest in emigration in 1802–1803, but, in doing so, provoked an outcry from most sectors of Scottish society. He argued that emigration was a rational and understandable reaction to the sweeping changes taking place in the Highlands and Islands. But he was very much a lone voice.[2] Most people with influence regarded emigration as a threat, arguing that it would deprive the nation of people who would otherwise be in its workforce or be military recruits, and did everything in their power to thwart the emigration movement. Emigration at the time was almost an act of defiance. People emigrated in spite of the barriers placed in their way. They were certainly not being encouraged to emigrate by their landlords nor was there any question, at this stage, of compulsion.

Selkirk was a lone figure who correctly read the mood of the people. Most Highlanders had to choose between an uncertain future if they stayed put or move, which effectively meant taking up a job in the manufacturing Lowlands or emigrating. Selkirk knew that, faced with that sort of choice, many who could afford their shipping fares would opt for emigration. Much to the dismay of Scotland's ruling classes, whole communities in the Highlands and Islands took the decision to emigrate and did so *en masse.* The prospect of a better life overseas as transplanted, culturally intact communities proved to be an awesomely compelling goal.

At first glance this was a surprising development. The Highlands and Islands of Scotland can hardly be said to be an obvious training ground for the North American outback. It is hard to imagine a less likely region. These are areas with few or no trees and with land which can only support extremely restricted agriculture. Yet these people did succeed, because as Selkirk correctly judged, their background made them particularly adept at coping with the hardships and isolation of life in the wilderness. He knew that a strong resolve and inner spirit fashioned by a tough climate and exacting living conditions determined staying power far more than practical skills. Their predilection for self-sufficiency made them ideal pioneers. But there was another important factor as well. The Western Isles and parts of the northwest Highlands had been losing colonisers to the southern colonies—particularly North Carolina from about 1770—some thirty years before Selkirk appeared on the scene.

In fact, the group of 800 or so who joined Selkirk's colonising scheme in 1802–1803 were relative latecomers to Prince Edward Island. By the time they arrived in Belfast, three other Scottish com-

munities had already established themselves on the north side of the
Island and they had been there from the early 1770s. The first two
groups which came to Stanhope (lot 34) and Malpeque (lot 18) in 1770
subsequently developed a strong Scottish presence, but each drew its
settlers from quite different parts of Scotland. Most of the Stanhope
Scots came from Perthshire and most Malpeque Scots came from
Argyll. Then there was the third contingent, which arrived two years
later in 1772 and took up holdings in Scotchfort (lot 36). They too had
their own particular identity, originating as they did from Catholic
strongholds in the Western Isles and west Inverness-shire.[3] Tombstones in these three locations also profess the geographical origins of
the many generations of Scots who contributed to the development of
these early settlements.

Our knowledge and understanding of Prince Edward Island's Scottish heritage is limited by the fact that so much previous work has centred around specific early settlements. Previous research has tended to
concentrate on the large groups which arrived in the 1770s and the
early 1800s, highlighting in particular the ancestry and activities of the
prominent families who took up land holdings. However exhaustive
such studies are, even when taken together, they only account for a
small fraction of the total number of Scots who emigrated during the
late eighteenth and nineteenth centuries. We therefore fail to take in
the total picture. A further difficulty comes from the nature of the surviving documentation. Overall, it is sparse and events are largely seen
through the eyes of the proprietors and church leaders who organised
the initial exodus of the emigrants and assisted in their settling in
process. Because most emigrants left little behind by way of the written word, we have only other people's views on their experiences as
settlers.

Although imperfect, we do have at our disposal two important historical sources which give us an overview of what happened to most
Scots who settled on the Island. The first is the 1881 Census of the
Island which required people to state their ethnic origins and religious
affiliations. In other words this Prince Edward Island Census tells us

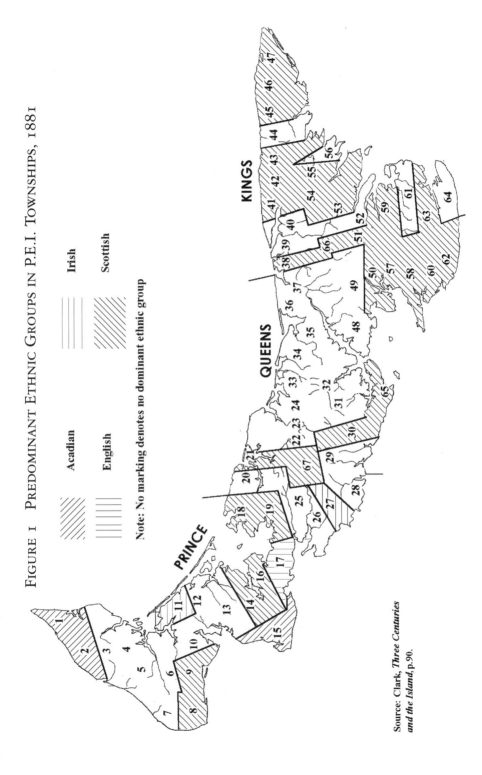

FIGURE 1 PREDOMINANT ETHNIC GROUPS IN P.E.I. TOWNSHIPS, 1881

Acadian

English

Irish

Scottish

Note: No marking denotes no dominant ethnic group

PRINCE

QUEENS

KINGS

Source: Clark, *Three Centuries and the Island*, p. 90.

where people claiming Scottish ancestry in 1881 were actually located (Figure 1).[4] We can see that there were strongly Presbyterian communities in the Belfast area and large concentrations of Roman Catholic Scots in Kings County, where remarkably some 61 per cent of the population claimed Scottish ancestry.[5] By 1881, the original Belfast nucleus (lots 57 and 58) had spread into six complete townships, giving Scots an overwhelming dominance over other ethnic groups in the south east of the Island. But this was certainly not the picture at Stanhope (lot 34) or Scotchfort (lot 36) which had begun life as solely Scottish footholds over a century earlier. Here, subsequent generations of Scots and Scottish-born arrivals simply merged into the background as they settled alongside the other English, Irish and native-born people who came to both places. Malpeque (lot 18) on the other hand, preserved a strongly Scottish identity, but the major clusters of Scottish settlers in this area of the Island developed not at Malpeque, but some distance to the southeast, closer to Charlottetown. Local place names—such as New Argyle (lot 65), Argyll Shore (lot 30) and Breadalbane (lot 67) hint at county origins and strongly confirm what the Census Returns tell us.

While the Census data enables us to identify those areas of the Island to which emigrant Scots were primarily drawn, we are still in the dark about the sequence of events which created these overall patterns. We only see a composite picture, built up over several decades, of the settlement choices of people claiming Scottish ancestry. The Census tells us nothing about where in Scotland the emigrants came from; nor does it tell us when they arrived. Fortunately we have a second source which comes from the emigrants themselves—their tombstone inscriptions and newspaper death notices. Pride in Scottish roots appears to have extended to the grave as countless emigrant Scots left death records behind of their loved ones, giving their earlier location in Scotland and year of arrival on the Island. This data has been gathered together for publication by the Prince Edward Island Genealogical Society. Their publication, containing the transcriptions of tombstones and death notices for over 750 Scots who died on the

The tombstone, inscribed in Gaelic, of Calum MacLeod located in
a tiny road-side cemetery in Belfast. *Photograph by I.G. Campey.*

Island between 1835 and 1910, is a rich source of data on the geographical origins of emigrant Scots.[6]

The Genealogical Society's publication does not claim to be com-
prehensive in its coverage and death notices and tombstones were certainly not universal happenings, but in spite of these limitations it pro-
vides us with an important window into the Island's Scottish past.[7]
Through it we see the potency of family and kinship ties as we observe
the large clusters of people, originating from the same areas of Scotland,
who chose to reside together in different parts of the Island. We can ask
why they selected the locations on the Island which they did. Knowing
where people settled leads us to a closer understanding of emigrant
motivations and expectations. Emigrants who chose populated places
with above average economic and job prospects were probably driven
primarily by entrepreneurial factors and a will to succeed. Emigrants

who chose locations where they could join others who shared their geographical origins were probably more driven by a desire to preserve their culture and identity. For the latter, emigration may have just been the least bad option, but for the former, it was a quest for a better life.

We have other documentary sources at our disposal as well. The much sought after passenger list often gives details of the places where emigrants originated but sadly, only a handful survive and these only cover the early periods of emigration from 1771 to 1808 (Appendix I).[8] Shipping sources which give head counts of passengers on particular ships give us another insight into people movements. If shipping records tell us of a Prince Edward Island bound ship which docked at Thurso on the north coast of Sutherland to collect a group of emigrants, then we know that we must look for arrivals from Sutherland to the Island during that particular year. Although reliable statistics on passengers who departed from Scottish ports for Prince Edward Island only appear regularly in official government reports from 1840, before this time we can sometimes obtain random data from newspaper reports.[9] Another less obvious and little used source of passenger data are the Scottish customs records which were kept for individual ports. Because both the food stores loaded on board for emigrants and the luggage were exempt from duty, officials needed to record them as separate items in the list kept of exports going out on a particular ship. Scottish customs records therefore often contain so-called "victualing bills," which record food provisions for the crew and a stated number of passengers, and they sometimes quantify the long lists of the chests, bags, bundles, barrels and trunks which constituted "passenger baggage."

A critical factor in the number of ships available was the North American timber trade, whose arrival completely revolutionised emigrant transport. Prince Edward Island and eastern Nova Scotia had been attracting Clyde shippers and merchants from the 1790s, albeit on a small scale. However, what began as a specialist trade in large oak and pine masts to the navy, rapidly changed into a general trade during the Napoleonic War years. The 1806 blockade of the Baltic cut off

FIGURE 2   CONCENTRATIONS OF SCOTTISH SETTLERS IN THE MARITIMES,
          1851–1871

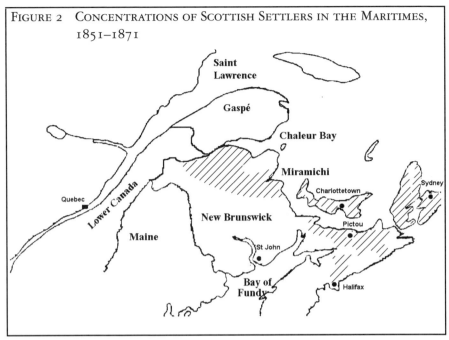

Maritime census data taken from: (i)   Clark, *Three Centuries and the Island*, 90;
                                 (ii) Clark, "Old World Origins and Religious
                                       Adherence to Nova Scotia," 320;
                                 (iii) Ganong, "Settlements, New Brunswick" 76

normal supplies to Britain for a period; but it was the doubling of the
already high duties on European wood in 1811 which had the more
dramatic and long-term effect.[10] The duties on Baltic timber increased
to the point where it was priced out of the market. In spite of the
greater distance to North America, timber from that source became
the cheaper alternative for British merchants. As a consequence, Maritime timber exports soared and as they did, shippers advertised for
passengers on their westward journeys. Shipowners built up regular
shipping services based on a two-way trade in timber and people.
Competition opened up between shippers and emigrants benefited
from the relatively low fares.[11]

     When timber importers claimed that the principal benefit to emi-
grants of the North American timber trade was cheap transport and

steady winter employment for settlers, they very much understated their case. The search for timber actually forged new shipping routes between Scotland and North America which had not previously existed. This in turn created opportunities for colonisers. As the search for timber supplies moved along the Northumberland Strait in the late eighteenth century, so too came the advance of Scottish settlers to Prince Edward Island, Cape Breton, eastern Nova Scotia and the Miramichi and Chaleur Bay regions of New Brunswick (Figure 2). The fact that this area attracted so many from the northwest Highlands and Islands during the late 1700s and early 1800s is largely attributable to the relative ease with which they could be collected by the many timber ships which were then leaving the Clyde. The timber trade was the sole reason why ships left in such numbers from Scottish ports and without those ships the early Scottish take over of the eastern Maritimes could not have happened.

Once emigrant successes in Prince Edward Island were relayed back to Scotland, emigration became an irresistible force, which no amount of government propaganda could halt.[12] The so-called "spirit of emigration" developed a will of its own and continued its acceleration after 1816, when the extreme poverty of the post-Napoleonic War years sparked off further emigration surges to the eastern Maritimes. The principal intake of Scots who came to the Island during this time originated from the Western Isles, the northwest Highlands and Dumfriesshire. A steady trickle continued to arrive in the 1820s, but Scots increasingly found themselves overtaken in numeric terms by the growing number of Irish immigrants who were being attracted to the Island. However, this trickle suddenly turned to a deluge during the late 1820s and early 1830s as the combined effects of the collapse of the kelp industry, a succession of bad harvests and the general industrial depression took its toll.[13] Large numbers from the Western Isles, particularly from Lord MacDonald's estate in Skye came to settle at Uigg (lot 50), close to the Belfast settlements which had been established some thirty years earlier in 1803. A second large group arrived in the early 1840s, as worsening economic conditions again

'Chain of migration' [handwritten marginal note]

stimulated emigration from Lord MacDonald's estate in Skye and they too headed for the Belfast area of the Island.

By the time that these later contingents from Skye arrived on the Island, attitudes to emigration had undergone an amazing transformation. With the severe depression which followed the Napoleonic Wars, emigration increasingly changed from being seen as a threat to becoming a cure-all for the nation's social ills. By the 1820s Highland proprietors, who had formerly fought hard to retain their tenants, increasingly swung around in favour of emigration schemes, although they largely resisted calls to finance their tenants' travel costs until the 1840s. The government too increasingly came under pressure to financially assist poor people to emigrate. It largely resisted such calls, but it had regularly to bow to public pressure to provide easy settlement terms to emigrants. The conflict between the proponents of efficient colonisation and those who viewed emigration merely as a means of disposing of Britain's surplus population dragged on for many years.[14] As these events showed, Lord Selkirk had been well ahead of his time when, decades earlier, he had advocated that those who wished to emigrate should be encouraged to do so on the grounds that it would send much-needed people to British North America and save people from the consequences of destitution.[15]

Landlords responded to the collapse of kelp markets and the general economic depression by restructuring their estates and turning more and more of their land over to sheep farms. Although the forces at work which led such large numbers to transfer from the Isle of Skye to Uigg in Prince Edward Island were clearly landlord induced, it should not be assumed that these emigrants necessarily came across with a heavy heart or under any duress. By the late 1820s most people in Skye, and elsewhere in the Highlands, would have been reconciled to the inevitability of on-going agricultural change. Large-scale removals were becoming a fact of life and for most it was a question of considering alternatives, not resisting the inevitable. Those who were amenable to the idea of emigration sought places to settle overseas and help to finance their journeys. A pre-existing Skye-dominated settlement in the shape of Belfast, coupled with the generous terms offered by their landlord, Lord MacDonald, would have been powerful inducements. Although most people might have preferred not to have been forced to choose other alternatives, the fact that so many came to this one area of Prince Edward Island demonstrates the enormous pulling power of a friendly face and strong community ties.

Understandably, Highland emigration to British America during the 1840s and 1850s has strong associations with the evictions and clearances which were so prevalent during this period. A significant factor linking the two was the passing of the 1845 Poor Law Amendment Act, which, for the first time, made landlords liable for poor tenants on their estates. This caused many landlords to look to emigration as the solution to this dilemma and, by offering to fund their tenants' removal costs, they hoped to achieve a result which suited their own pockets and the future interests of their tenantry.[16] But it is the dark days of the Highland Famine Years, from 1846 to 1856, years associated with widespread clearances and a huge increase in emigration, which stand out most. There were, undoubtedly, some instances of forced or determinedly executed evictions linked with emigration during these few years. But it should be noted that these were exceptional and extreme cases. Sadly, in more recent times, these events have come to be taken as typical of the sinister forces which allegedly pervaded emigration, spawning a victim culture which is closer to mythology than fact.

m'neills of Colonsay

As with the rest of British America, the Scottish invasion of Prince Edward Island left behind a string of successes. The typical Scot who came to the Island was driven by his own personal agenda and was not solely reacting to events at home. He was not a passive victim of harsh forces, but was instead an independent spirit who, having chosen to emigrate, found the money for his own fares and carefully decided on his destination. But the most important feature of our typical Scot is his timing. Scots became residents of Prince Edward Island far earlier than their Irish and English counterparts. Until the start of the Napoleonic Wars in 1803, Scots were dominant on the Island as well as in many other parts of British America. In Prince Edward Island they built up something like a 50 year lead over Irish and English settlers. People of Scottish ancestry remained the dominant group in many areas of the Island for decades, but the relatively high intake of Irish immigrants from the 1820s steadily altered the ethnic balance in favour of the Irish. On the basis of first generation only, Irish ancestry and not Scottish ancestry was predominant from the late 1840s.[17]

Scots came in large numbers at a time, in the late eighteenth and early nineteenth centuries, when their resolve to emigrate had to withstand the verbal battering they received from the Scottish establishment who fiercely opposed emigration. Yet so much emphasis has been placed on the economic and social factors which may have forced desperate people to seek a new life abroad, that the possibility that emigrants may have actually had some positive reasons for wishing to emigrate is rarely considered.[18] Scots were enormously successful pioneers and acquired a high reputation for their farming and entrepreneurial skills, not just in Prince Edward Island but in many of the farthest corners of the world.

Nothing was ever handed to these people on a silver plate. It took great courage, resilience and determination to become a successful pioneer. Even those who were fleeing the poverty of the post-war period, following the Napoleonic Wars, took a considered view of where they wanted to settle and went about planning their departure and land purchase arrangements with considerable care and efficiency. Yet their story is so heavily doom-laden. Even tales of their ship voyages are usually laced with negative imagery. As is discussed in the final chapter, here too perceptions have been unduly pessimistic. Emigrants were not generally taken across the sea on leaking broken down boats, as is commonly thought, but were in fact usually offered the latest and best shipping available. Through the use of wide-ranging historical sources we now attempt to trace their journey from Scotland to the Island, unravel their choice of location on it and consider why they chose the places they did.

II

The First Arrivals from Scotland

"Archibald Ramsay, Esq., of Beach Point, a native of Argyleshire, Scotland, who emigrated to this Island in 1770, died March 10, 1839, aged 83. Also his wife Helen, a native of the same place who emigrated in 1771, died 20 June 1853 aged 85. They were both members of the Presbyterian Church..." [18–2–565][1]

WHEN A MILITARY officer's family from Campbeltown succeeded in obtaining a half share of lot 18 at Malpeque Bay in 1767, Argyll people, like Archibald and Helen Ramsay, found themselves with a local contact through whom they could secure land in Prince Edward Island. Because he drew most of his recruits from his native Argyll, he and his followers were the catalysts behind Malpeque Bay's strong and enduring Argyll links. This pattern was repeated twice more during the 1770s when two prominent Scots, one from Perthshire and the other from Inverness-shire, with land to settle on the Island, found their willing emigrants from their own part of Scotland. Prince Edward Island's early development as a British colony thus took place as a series of highly organised ventures which were planned and financed by proprietors. Scottish proprietors were more inclined than most to seek settlers for their land acquisitions on the Island. To appreciate why this was so we need first to look back over the Island's early formative period as a British colony.

Britain acquired the Island of St. John (renamed Prince Edward Island) from the French in 1763 and, having done so, more or less immediately granted out tracts of its land to people who were thought to deserve the patronage of the British Crown. Prince Edward Island's fate was, to some extent, a natural outcome of colonial policies, which gave Britain's mercantile and defensive concerns a priority over all others. Throughout North America, it had been common for the government to treat land as a reward for services rendered, whether in the battlefield or high office, thus ensuring that vast tracts, of often the best land, went to people who were usually more interested in cutting business deals than in tilling the soil as settlers. Prince Edward Island stands alone in being the only colony to have its entire territory sold off with a sweep of the imperialistic hand. Thus it was that the Island was taken out of the reach of ordinary settlers and given to a privileged few, most of whom had little interest in settling the land or in the long-term future of the Island's economic prosperity.

Military expediency was the driving force behind the government's interest in the region. Initially, the northern colonies had little to offer apart from fish and fur, but by acquiring them, Britain could consolidate her hold over her much more highly-prized southern colonies. Even though they were not as highly regarded, these more northerly possessions needed to have loyal settlers and a steadily growing population if they were to remain in British hands. This strategy, of course, meant that indigenous populations had first to be removed. As was the case in the rest of the Maritime region, Prince Edward Island's Native Peoples were progressively removed from their lands and the French-speaking Acadians had to surrender their territory to the British. Although they were initially expelled in 1755, many Acadians later returned, but were restricted to remote areas and relatively poor land.[2]

Overshadowing Britain's colonial policies was a long-standing determination that population growth in the colonies would be achieved at minimum cost to the public purse. The government's policy therefore had been to devolve colonisation costs as much as possible to interested third parties—usually wealthy landowners or merchants. So the reasoning behind the government's decision to grant all of Prince Edward Island's land to wealthy proprietors was based on the belief that the proprietors, not the government, would have to finance the various schemes needed to attract settlers.[3] However clever this strategy may have looked in Whitehall, it failed abysmally. The lottery to determine who of the claimants would get which portion of land went ahead in 1767. In a single day, the Island was surveyed and divided into 67 townships (or lots of about 20,000 acres), each of which was granted arbitrarily to various claimants, irrespective of their suitability or motives.[4] Most proprietors failed to make any payments or meet their settlement obligations. There were no effective sanctions and the result was that the Island became saddled with a divisive and dysfunctional land system for the best part of one hundred years.[5] Throughout this time, settlers faced a murky world of land dealers and absentee landlords, who effectively held power but yet felt no sense of responsibility for the well-being of the Island.

Not surprisingly, then, the population grew slowly. The population was only 1,300 in the late 1770s and 49 of the 67 lots had no settlers at all. Some thirty years after the lottery, the Island could claim only 4,400 inhabitants and, by the end of the century, 23 lots remained completely uninhabited.[6] Nearly all of the proprietors were just sitting back waiting for their land to increase in value and, in the meantime, sought people willing to take up leaseholds on their land. Those emigrants who came to the Island thus had to comply with a near-feudal land system which made them tenants rather than freeholders, and gave them little prospect of ever converting their capital into land.[7] However, Scots were not deterred by the Island's feudal tendencies and were first on the scene from Britain. They had shown a similar zeal for emigration some decades earlier when the southern colonies beckoned. From the mid-eighteenth century large numbers from the Highlands and Islands had gone to settle in North Carolina and New York and now in 1770, with the opening up of Prince Edward Island to British settlers, they had another option to consider.[8]

The forces driving the exodus of people had been powerful and diverse. The collapse of the traditional clan system following the Jacobite rebellions of 1715 and 1745, the persecution of Roman Catholics, agricultural reform and severe economic depressions all played their part, as did the Scottish propensity for enterprise and military service. While the combined effects of over-population together with relatively poor soil productivity would have been significant causes of disquiet in themselves, it was the major disruption caused by the advancing sheep farms which created the large emigration surges of the late eighteenth and early nineteenth centuries. Most came initially from remote areas in the northwest of Scotland, where living conditions were at their most precarious and alternatives to emigration in least supply. Perthshire and Argyll were among the first to feel the pull of emigration, having extensive sheep farms from the 1770s, while Ross-shire and West Inverness-shire experienced the advance from the following decade. Another factor was persecution against Roman Catholics, which proved an even more powerful force than the advancing sheep farms in some parts of the Western Isles and west Inverness-shire. The tenants of South Uist of the MacDonald estate were put under great pressure by their Laird to convert to Presbyterianism. The tenants who were mainly Roman Catholics resisted but were still harassed by their Laird. This culminated in their decision to emigrate. They were led by John MacDonald of Glenadale who was assisted by the behind the scenes efforts of Bishop John MacDonald, the Scottish Roman Catholic Bishop of that area.

The combined effects of agricultural change and religion were thus important propelling forces behind emigration. In all, three Scottish settlements were launched in Prince Edward Island within five years of the lottery having taken place. The Island's location was an obvious attraction. It was one of the nearest parts of North America to Scotland, giving it a clear advantage in terms of travel costs. Oddly enough, the Island's notorious proprietorial system went with the grain of Scottish attitudes to emigration. The natural inclination of most Scots was to emigrate in groups and to seek someone to manage and finance them. Well-resourced proprietors were a godsend since they could

Stanhope memorial to commemorate the arrival of the
Falmouth passengers from Greenock in 1770. *Courtesy of
Stanhope Historical Society.*

provide financial backing for their journeys and their first few years on
the Island. The successful and early domination of the Island by Scots
thus owes much to their strongly communal approach. If living under
a proprietor's wing meant the denial of freehold land it was, at least in
the short-term, a price worth paying. The arrangement suited Scottish
proprietors as well, since they could transpose semi-feudal Scottish
tenancies to the Island, and see a return on capital invested.

Two groups left Scotland for the Island in 1770. The first consisted of
60 men, mainly from Perthshire, who sailed on the *Falmouth* from
Greenock. Their proprietor was the Lord Advocate of Scotland, James
Montgomery, who sought to establish a flax plantation on his newly
acquired land at Stanhope (lot 34).[9] He employed David Lawson, an
experienced flax farmer from Callander to recruit suitable emigrants on
his behalf and later to run the plantation. Because Lawson did his recruit-
ing locally, most emigrants shared his Perthshire origins. Montgomery
put up most of the money for the venture and employed the emigrants

as indentured servants, using their labour for four years in return for a
free passage and leaseholds at the end of the expiry period. He probably
got little back on his cash advances, which ran to over £1,200. Thus,
judged as a money-making exercise, the venture was a failure.

Although unintentional, Montgomery did have some impact as an
emigration promoter. As a pillar of the Scottish establishment, a group
that at the time was hell-bent on stopping North American emigration, he could hardly appear to be supporting widespread emigration
from Perthshire. But if Montgomery was going to make a profit from
his land in Prince Edward Island he needed to find willing recruits.
He resolved his dilemma by instructing his plantation manager to
recruit men only, and not families, and to run his affairs "in such a
manner as to incur as little observation as possible."[10] In spite of
Montgomery's best efforts to curtail emigration, Perthshire's links with
the Island grew and prospered. Although many men left the Stanhope
area when their indentures expired, some did stay and took up their
land grants.[11] Privations and difficulties were experienced initially but
ultimately favourable reports attracted the many Perthshire emigrants
who arrived at Stanhope and Beaton Point (lot 47) in the early 1800s.
As confidence in the Island's benefits grew, still more came and, by
1809, New Perth (lot 52) had been founded.[12]

The second group to leave Scotland in 1770 were Argyll emigrants,
led and partially financed by Lieutenant Colonel Robert Stewart. He
was a relatively small investor, who was probably looking for a modest income to supplement his army pension. Estimates vary, but it is
likely that the *Annabella,* whose passengers were later described as
being "housed happy and contented" and the *Edinburgh* of Campbeltown, which left Campbeltown in 1770 and 1771 respectively, carried between them around 60 families.[13] This was very much a Stewart family undertaking. The Lieutenant Colonel's brother-in-law, also
called Robert Stewart and his family travelled on the *Annabella* with
the emigrants, and stayed behind to organise their resettlement. A surviving passenger list for the *Edinburgh* tells us that the Lieutenant
Colonel's brother, Peter, who later became a Chief Justice of the

Island, paid the fares of several families who arrived in 1771.[14]

As with the Stanhope venture, the early years brought horrific problems for the emigrants and great disappointment to Stewart, particularly as he had the misfortune to lose his and his groups' supplies. Some of the Argyll emigrants immediately moved across to a nearby abandoned Acadian site on the west side of Malpeque Bay (lot 13) in order to avoid the clearing operations which still needed to be undertaken at lot 18. But, in spite of this shaky start, both sides of Malpeque Bay were to preserve their Scottish identity and by 1813 the area had acquired its first Presbyterian Church.[15] However, although the Argyll connections with Malpeque Bay remained strong, it was the Argyll Islands of Mull and Colonsay which ultimately provided the major outflow of people to the Island. As we shall see in a later chapter, the Argyll Islanders who began arriving from the early 1800s did not opt for Malpeque but instead chose to be closer to the Island's economic heartland, settling just to the west of Charlottetown. Unlike the 1770 groups from the Argyll mainland, who were organised and led by a proprietor, the Mull and Colonsay emigrants were self-managed and financed. A crucial development, which gave these and others like them increased independence, was the emergence of regular shipping from the Scotland to the Island as timber exports from the eastern Maritime forests to Britain began to soar.

But it was the third group, Gaelic-speaking Roman Catholics from the Western Isles and west Inverness-shire who initially made the largest impact on the Island. Although religious persecution lay behind the emigration surge of 1772, the emigrants had by no means come to a place which offered religious sanctuary. They were the *persona non grata* of the Island from the moment they stepped from their ships. A greater departure from the government's preferred English-speaking, Church of England immigrant stereotype is difficult to imagine. Of course, at a time when prejudices ran very deep, not just in Britain but throughout the colonies, Roman Catholics had to contend with widespread discrimination wherever they went. In Prince Edward Island they were not even legally permitted to hold land until the 1780s, nor could they be counted as settlers in terms of fulfilling proprietor settlement obligations.[16] But officials and ministers back in London could rant and rave all they liked about the characteristics of the ideal emigrant. In the end the choice of person was not theirs. It was a case of self-selection, determined by the emigrants themselves. The Roman Catholic Highlanders stayed and the arrival of even larger numbers to the Island during the 1790s speaks for itself.

The 1772 group came as a result of an initiative taken by Captain John MacDonald of Glenaladale, a prominent tacksman, who purchased Scotchfort (lot 36) with the assistance of the Catholic Church, which at the time, wanted Scottish lairds to improve conditions for their tenants. Having high social standing within the Scottish feudal system, tacksmen like John MacDonald were authoritative figures who commanded considerable respect from estate tenants.[17] Scotchfort was one of Sir James Montgomery's townships and had been obtained with the assistance of Bishop John MacDonald. The Catholic Church, which preferred to stay in the background, helped to find funds for the few families who were unable to pay their own passages. The two hundred or so Catholic Highlanders, who sailed to the Island in 1772 on the *Alexander* of Greenock, came mainly from the Catholic strongholds within the MacDonald estates, especially in South Uist, Barra, Eigg and mainland west Inverness-shire. While Scotchfort was the principal destination for these settlers, death notices tell us that some, like Donald Beaton from Lochaber, slipped away to the eastern most tip, Beaton Point (lot 47), to establish a second Catholic foothold on the Island.[18]

The troubles had their origin in the ill-feeling created within the MacDonald estate when the South Uist tenantry were put under pressure to convert to Presbyterianism. The changing economic conditions which most threatened the tacksman class were an added spur to their leader, who dispatched his brother off to America to look for land.[19] John MacDonald had reservations about the venture but was in a hopeful mood just before he embarked:

"Emigrations that were carrying on in Argyleshire about Campbelton, opened my eyes to the like Schemes and my brother chancing to come home and taking descriptions and plans we saw of the Island of Saint John in the Gulf of St. Lawrence, we both purchased at a venture from the Lord Advocate Mr. Montgomery the best lot to appearance of the whole Island.

Our method is to give them by lease forever, a certain number of acres, such as they can manage easily then paying us a small quitrent out of it and furnishing themselves all necessaries and passage, only that we must assist them to carry it on …. It is a most expensive project requiring a vast sight of ready money, but I hope to get it gone through, though with difficulty."[20]

The news fed back the following year, by the Catholic priest, who accompanied the passengers on the *Alexander,* that people are likely to remain "in great misery" if they stayed on the Island must have given cause for concern. However, by the next year Bishop John MacDonald had better news to report:

"We received lately accounts from Saint John by several letters even from the malcontents as give sufficient room to hope that this undertaking will thrive."[21]

The wartime conditions from 1775 to 1783, the years of the American Revolution, greatly impeded the Island's trade and economic life although it, itself, was never involved in any conflict. Placing Scotchfort in the hands of his sisters, for the day-to-day running of his property, John MacDonald of Glenaladale went off to fight on the British side in the Royal Highlands Emigrants Regiment (or 84th as it was known) taking some of his tenants with him. Upon his return to Scotchfort after the war, he faced demands from some of the Catholic districts in the Hebrides and west Inverness-shire for help in obtaining land on the Island. By the early 1790s, the area was fast becoming a considerable Catholic enclave, particularly when MacDonald later, in 1792, managed to acquire the lot adjoining Scotchfort, at lot 35.

First came the *Jane* and *Lucy* in 1790 with a total of 238 passengers, mainly from Moidart, Morar, Eigg and South Uist.[22] The following year, the *Royal Gazette* could hardly contain its excitement at the impending arrival of the: "four hundred of the sons and daughters of famed Caledonia [who] have embarked for this flourishing Island."[23] Further details followed upon the safe arrival of the 1791 contingent of Roman Catholics from the Clanranald estates in South Uist:

> "It is with singular pleasure we announce the arrival of those honest and worthy Caledonian emigrants…. There is not a doubt but they will receive a kind reception, and experience that hospitality which so characteristically and eminently distinguishes the Highland race."[24]

They had sailed on the *Mally* and *Queen* of Greenock, which together carried a total of 536 passengers. Given that these ships were of only modest size, overcrowding must have been severe, although complaints centred on fuel and food (Appendix 2). The *Gazette* reported that "the *Mally* was without fuel part of the passage and her water so bad that it was scarcely possible to use it." However, it also reported that passengers carried by the *Queen* "speak handsomely of the kind treatment they received from Captain Morrison. His conduct is worthy of being followed by all masters of vessels."[25] But, however kind the Captain may have been, these were September arrivals, who were being given scarcely any time to brace themselves for their first North American winter.

Conditions were extremely tough and because of their late arrival, emigrants were dependant on assistance over the winter. Early reports spoke of half-starved, freezing, disillusioned people who were desperately unhappy with their plight:

> "This province is terrible cold, we have seven months of snow and frost and sometimes eight…we came here we thought ourselves to make money but we came to freeze instead."[26]

Back in Scotland, the bleak reports of struggling emigrants were fil-
tering back and were seized upon with great enthusiasm by the opponents of emigration, who gave them as wide a circulation as possible.
But the advocates of emigration fought back. In 1794, the *Royal
Gazette* contained an article about someone called Andrew, a man
from Barra who came to the Island with his family and in just four
years achieved "the happy effects which in this country constantly flow
from sobriety and industry when united with good land and freedom."
Andrew was probably a fictional character and the stories of his pleasing encounters in Charlottetown a complete fabrication, but such
journalistic efforts demonstrate that emigration propagandists had
their black arts too:

> "Several citizens impelled either by spontaneous attachments or
> motives of humanity took many of them [the emigrants] to their
> houses; the city agreeably to its usual wisdom and humanity ordered
> them all to be lodged in the barracks and plenty of provisions giv-
> en them.... He gazed with uninterrupted attention on everything he
> saw; the house, the inhabitants, the negroes and carriages...."[27]

So, as a result of economic and religious tensions in Scotland, Prince
Edward Island acquired large numbers of Gaelic-speaking Catholics
in the last three decades of the eighteenth century. Thus Gaelic, not
English initially became the dominant language of the Island. This outcome had certainly not been the original intention of the Roman
Catholic Church which had merely wanted to force better conditions
at home. Instead the Scottish Church had to look on with dismay as
more of its congregations and clergymen were swept away by the emigration movement.[28] Part of the reason for the huge response was their
initial leader, John MacDonald of Glenaladale. Although in later years
he became a rather controversial and isolated figure, thus stemming
his overall influence on the social and political development of the
Island, his high status in the eyes of his Highland followers made him
a pivotal character during the early stages of emigration.

Painting of Reverend Angus Bernard MacEachern,
first Bishop of Charlottetown, artist unknown. *Courtesy of Diocese of Charlottetown, PEI Public Archives
and Records Office, 2320/70–3.*

Prince Edward Island was not the only beneficiary of the large exodus
from Catholic regions of the Scottish Highlands and Islands. By 1793,
large numbers of Catholic Scots were also to be found at Arisaig, Nova
Scotia, which was located more or less directly opposite the Scottish
Catholic concentrations in Prince Edward Island. Anxious that the
new Catholic arrivals should not be lost to the missionary endeavours
of the local Presbyterian minister at Pictou, Father Angus MacEachern (later Bishop), who was based in Prince Edward Island at the time,
persuaded many Catholic newcomers to settle in, or near Arisaig, or

in Cape Breton. Thanks largely to his efforts, therefore, Scottish Catholics were effectively concentrated in one single part of the Maritimes, albeit one which was divided by stretches of water. When he eventually took over this sprawling parish in 1807 from Father James MacDonald, Father MacEachern was able to oversee a thriving Catholic population lying within a compact triangle, taking in the east side of Prince Edward Island, the eastern end of the mainland and large areas of Cape Breton.[29]

Although Scotchfort began its days in the 1770s as a great centre of Catholic Highland settlement, its appeal quickly wore thin as subsequent waves of settlers rejected tenancies in favour of land ownership. Scotchfort retained its strongly Catholic affiliations, but in time Scots lost their dominance and had to share lot 36 with Irish Catholics. In fact from as early as 1790, Scotchfort operated as a type of staging post for Highland Catholics. It was the place where new arrivals got their bearings, not the place where most settled permanently. Some opted for a new life in Cape Breton, while others tried to get their own land in nearby townships, usually by squatting. Many of the 1790–1791 arrivals settled at lots 37 and 38, along the Hillsborough River, while others chose sites further to the southeast, along the Cardigan River (lot 54), at Launching (lot 55), and Little Pond (lot 56). Another option was Beaton Point (lot 47), which had been colonised by Highland Catholics from as early as 1772. Thus there was a steady outflow of Scottish Catholics marching steadily eastwards from Scotchfort and another one moving in the opposite direction from Beaton Point. There was also another link with the past. As a result of the 1767 lottery, lots 38, 39, 41 and 42 had fallen into the hands of some officers from the disbanded Fraser Highlanders (78th). It is highly likely that these officers encouraged fellow Highlanders to take up at least some of this land, thus providing yet another Highland base on the east side of the Island.[30] Little wonder then, that Scots, who were mainly Roman Catholic, predominated in ten of the Kings County townships and did so until 1848 (lots 38, 41, 42, 43, 45, 46, 47, 53, 54, 55).[31]

Thus by the turn of the century Scots had laid claim to Malpeque,

Scotchfort Monument to commemorate the arrival of the first Scottish
Roman Catholic immigrants. The
inscription reads: AMDG (1772–
1922) "This cross marks the site of
the first Catholic Church erected in
Prince Edward Island after the Conquest. It is set up by the descendants
of the Scottish Catholic Pioneers to
perpetuate the memory of their
arrival in this country and to symbol-
ize the faith for the sake of which
they left their homes in Scotland and
became voluntary exiles amid the
wilds of Prince Edward Island."
*Courtesy of PEI Public Archives and
Records Office, Charlottetown Camera
Club Collection, Acc. 2320/3–9.*

Stanhope and large tracts of Kings County. But there were other emigrant groups who came to the Island in the eighteenth century who
failed to establish long-term settlements. The passengers from Dumfriesshire and Kirkcudbrightshire, who sailed on the *Lovelly Nelly* in
1774 and 1775, and together totalled 149, had the misfortune to arrive
on the Island at the beginning of the American Rebellion.[32] So too the
52 emigrants from Morayshire, who arrived in 1775, having sailed on
the *John and Elizabeth,* with the intention of settling on Samuel Smith's
land at lot 57.[33] Unlike the three major groups which preceded them,
who had the backing of proprietors both during their voyages and in
the early phases of relocation, the 1774–1775 arrivals were virtually
left to their own devices. They experienced horrendous problems, par-

ticularly in securing supplies during escalating wartime conditions. Lack of provisions and their remote location, far away from other settlers, demoralised the Morayshire group and they left without trace while most of the Dumfriesshire and Kirkcudbrightshire emigrants relocated themselves in Pictou, settling along the West River from Pictou Harbour.[34]

It is not at all surprising that dismal news of these ventures filtered back to Scotland. According to the local church minister, writing nearly 20 years later, in 1792, those who left New Abbey, in Kirkcudbrightshire "had abundant reason to repent leaving their native country" as did the people of Cummertrees in Dumfriesshire:

> "about forty people, some of them farmers but mostly labourers and tradesmen emigrated to America. They were enticed by advertisements sent by people who had acquired large tracts of land and wished to have it peopled...those who could afford to returned home."[35]

As events later showed, these gloomy accounts did not deter subsequent emigration from Dumfriesshire. However, there was a gap of about 40 years before emigration to Prince Edward from this region did resume. It was only when the southwest of Scotland developed its own timber trade links with the eastern Maritimes, which it did from 1816, that cheap and regular transatlantic shipping became available to emigrants.

Emigration from Scotland to the Island had reached new peaks in 1790–1791 and then again a decade later. During the intervening years the war between Britain and France, which began in 1793, curtailed emigration. With the resumption of a temporary peace in 1801, a rapid growth in emigration, particularly from the Highlands and Islands, was once again experienced. At around this time Prince Edward's Island's governing officials were trying to come to grips with the Island's chaotic land system and dismal record in attracting settlers. Some progress was made in identifying the extent of settlement in the various townships and in encouraging new proprietors to take over neglected townships, but the self-interest of proprietors continued to reign supreme.

Although the Island's failure to address its immigration and settlement requirements continued to hinder its development, it did have the good fortune to attract Lord Selkirk's financial backing and support. Appearing on the scene in 1803, Selkirk's contribution to the growth and success of Scottish settlements on the Island was truly immense. Gathering together an eight hundred strong contingent from the northwest Highlands and Islands, he took personal responsibility for the venture and presided over the establishment of settlements on some of the huge tracts of land that he had acquired by buying out other proprietors. Unlike them, Selkirk had a genuine interest *motives?* in the well-being of settlers and wanted them to prosper. As the following chapter demonstrates, they did succeed and would confound Selkirk's many critics.

III

THE SELKIRK SETTLERS OF 1803

"They were a very fine class of immigrants…They were an enterprising
and energetic people who transmitted their vigourous dispositions and
their stalwart physique to their children and their children's children.
Descendants of these settlers have been distinguished in almost every
walk of life…Their sons have distinguished themselves in every
profession, trade and pursuit…Lord Selkirk did well for this
Island when he brought these immigrants to its shores."[1]

THESE WORDS WERE written some 120 years after the arrival of the
initial group of Hebrideans to Belfast and is high praise indeed. Their
undoubted success owed much to the wealth, influence and practical
abilities of their leader and proprietor, Lord Selkirk. He had a real passion to see this scheme succeed and left nothing to chance. Rumblings
of discontent in the Hebrides, in the early 1800s, led him to Dr. Angus
MacAuley, a Gaelic-speaking academic and former factor on the Skye
estate of Lord MacDonald.[2] Although he met fierce resistance from
landholders in the Western Isles, Dr. MacAuley was extremely successful in signing up Highlanders for Selkirk's emigration venture,
finding many recruits from his previous employer's estate in Skye.
Angus MacAuley was ideally placed to attract large numbers in that
he could offer potential emigrants a complete package. He could allay
fears about the voyage, since he and Selkirk would be accompanying

the emigrants, was a credible and trusted negotiator, and he held out the prospect of a secure future, since he was a fellow emigrant and would be spending his remaining years on the Island. A charismatic man and natural leader, he commanded widespread respect and affection, combining the roles of schoolmaster, lay preacher and physician.[3]

Beginning his recruitment in 1802, Dr. MacAuley helped Selkirk to locate 800 people, mainly from the Hebrides, who set sail to the Island in the following year. Given his contacts in Skye, it would have been easy for Dr. MacAuley to identify people, particularly from the MacDonald estate, who were known to be thinking of emigrating. In 1802 John Campbell, Lord MacDonald's Edinburgh solicitor, had actually produced a list of his lordship's Skye tenants who were "going to America" (Table 1).[4] In fact, most of the names appearing in Campbell's list can be identified in a later, and incomplete listing of the initial settlers who went to Belfast in 1803 (Table 2).[5] MacAuley's intelligence sources and powers of persuasion were clearly finely tuned, since, based at least on this sample, Prince Edward Island's pulling power from this one area of Skye was quite exceptional. This outcome in some ways is surprising since Angus MacAuley's task was anything but simple.

Having been instructed initially by Selkirk to find potential emigrants for a settlement he proposed to found in Upper Canada, Dr. MacAuley had suddenly to re-negotiate the terms on offer. At the eleventh hour, the government, wishing to contain the rising tide of emigration, withdrew its support for Selkirk's Upper Canada scheme. The persistent Selkirk salvaged his venture by persuading the government to let him purchase land in Prince Edward Island instead. So, having sold local people on Upper Canada, Dr. MacAuley then had somehow to convince them that Prince Edward Island was an even better place.[6] His dilemma was not helped by the vociferous campaigning of Hebridean landowners, who were anxious to retain their tenantry for the lucrative profits to be made from kelp, or the fact that an earlier expedition from Morayshire to lot 57, the Belfast site, had ended in failure.[7] Fortunately for Selkirk, the impending introduction of the Passenger Act in 1803, focussed minds on the

Table 1: Tenants from Lord MacDonald's Estate in Skye who were intending to emigrate to America c.1802* [SRO GD 221/4433/1]

[* The full title begins: 'List of tenants who were to get lands by the arrangement made at Edinburgh and who are now going to emigrate to America.' There is no recorded date but the paper watermark can be dated to c. 1802. The list is signed by John Campbell, an Edinburgh lawyer in the employment of Lord MacDonald.]

Kendram
Going to America
1 Donald Nicolson
2 John Gillies
3 John Ross
4 Donald McLeod   ] After agreeing to take their lands, sold their
                       ] stock and mean to emigrate #
5 Rory McLeod

Balmacqueen
Going to America
6 John MacDonald

Peingown and Osmigarry
Going to America
7 John MacDonald

Peenorcronan
8 Donald Buchanan goes to America

Brogaig
9 Alexander Lamont goes to America

Balmeanach
10 Martin Martin goes to America

Stenscholl
11 John Nicolson goes to America

Clachan
12 Angus Betton goes to America

Maligar
13 Donald McLeod goes to America
14 Donald Dochardy goes to America
15 Malcolm McLeod goes to America

Upper Ollach
16 Donald MacSween goes to America #

Shulishadermor
17 John Nicolson goes to America, he was to have been turned out and John Beaton to go in his place.

[# All but Rory McLeod and Donald MacSween appear in the list of Selkirk settlers (Table 2); but assuming Donald MacSween is Donald MacQueen, he too can be found in Table 2.]

Table 2: Selkirk settlers residing at Belfast, in 1811 [PAPEI 2704/4]

Heads of Families

Rev. Dr Angus MacAulay

Murdoch Gillis*	Donald Gillis	Donald MacRae, Sr.
Donald MacRae	Evander MacRae*	Hector MacDonald
Murdoch MacLean	Donald MacKinnon	Donald Murchison*
Donald MacLeod	John Murchison	Donald Murchison
Alexr. McLeod	John McDonald Sr.*	John McDonald, Jr.
John Gillis	Donald Nicholson*	Murdo McLeod
Donald McPherson	Harry MacLeod	Saml. Martin
John Nicholson	Donald Nicholson	John McKenzie
John Campbell	John Ross	Donald Beaton
John Beaton	Donald Ross	Angus Beaton
Angus Ross	Samuel Beaton	John Gillis
Angus MacMillan	Chas. Stewart	Donald McInnes
Angus McDonald	Allen Shaw	John McLeod
Donald McPhee	John MacRae	Roderick MacRae
Donald MacRae	Kenneat McKinzie	Alexr. McKinzie
Hector Morrison	Donald McRae	Donald Stewart
Alexr. Martin	Charles Stewart	John MacPherson
John Bell	Lachlin MacLean	Malcolm Bell
Malcolm McMillan	James Cowrie	Donald McNeil
Malcolm Mun	Jas. Currie	Jas. Munn
Hector MacMillan	James MacMillan	Angus Mun
Allan MacMillan	Archibald Blue	Malcolm McNeill
Dugald Bell	John Mun	Angus Bell
John McPherson	Finley MacRae	Duncan MacRae
Peter Campbell	Angus Beaton, Sr	Kenneth McKenzie, Sr.
John MacRae	Finlay MacRae	Alex. McArthur
Alexr. McKenzie	John McDonald	Alex. McLeod
John McDonald	Malcolm MacLeod	Donald Martin
Donald MacLeod	Murdoch McDonald	Finly Odarty
Donald McLeod	Angus Odarchy	Donald Odochardy
Hector McQuary	John McLeod	John Buchanan
Murdoch Buchanan	John MacQueen	Alexr. Lamond
Martin Martin	Sairle Nicholson	Malcolm Buchanan
Donald Buchanan	Donald MacLeod	Donald MacQueen
Peter Murchison		

* Denotes Elder

The following note appears at the end of this list:
"This list is not a complete list of the Selkirk Settlers of 1803. No such list is known to exist. This was given to me as being signers of a letter to Rev. Dr. MacAulay in 1811, [in] appreciation of his services to the new community. This letter was turned over to me by Miss B. MacKinnon, daughter of Lieut. Governor D.A.McKinnon, himself a descendant of Selkirk.

Mary C.Brehaut"

higher prices which could be avoided, since he promised not to raise his fares.[8]

Most of the initial Belfast settlers were drawn from Skye, especially the east side of the Island where Lord MacDonald's lands were concentrated, and from the Clanranald estates in South Uist. Skye people maintained a long association with the Island, but this was not so with South Uist emigrants, who changed their allegiance to Nova Scotia and Cape Breton. Before becoming closely linked with the Island, Skye emigrants had earlier shown a marked preference for North Carolina.[9] It was said, at the time that they went to Prince Edward Island, that Skye was "a district which had so decided a connection with North Carolina that no emigrants had ever gone from it to any other quarter."[10] Indeed, Selkirk claimed that he had chosen people for his venture who would otherwise be lost to the United States. In successfully relocating his group of settlers, Selkirk was instrumental in dramatically changing the direction of the clannish pull from North Carolina to Prince Edward Island. He essentially moved it from south to north. The success of the Belfast venture meant that the Island became a powerful magnet for Skye settlers. No other part of British America attracted them in such large numbers.[11] Even by the 1830s and 1840s when all other parts of Scotland had long since rejected the Island on economic grounds, Skye emigrants continued to settle in the southeast part of the Island in their hundreds.

The initial group of 800 left Scotland in June, 1803 in three ships, the *Polly, Dykes* and *Oughton*.[12] Selkirk and around 200 people, mainly from Skye sailed on the *Dykes,* the best of the three ships, being only five years old and classed as an A1 (first-class) ship.[13] A second Skye party of around 400 sailed on the *Polly*, a forty-year-old ship, while a group from South Uist sailed on the *Oughton* which although not as old as the *Polly*, had been given a poorer rating at the time by the Lloyd's surveyors (Appendix 2). Selkirk probably located the *Polly* by placing this notice in the *Glasgow Courier:*

WANTED,

A VESSEL to carry 400 PASSEN-
GERS from PORTRIE in the ISLE
of SKY, to St. JOHN's or PICTOU,
NOVA SCOTIA, to be ready for fea by
the firſt of June. The owner of the veſ-
fel to be at the expence of fitting up births
furnifhing water cafks and water, with fuel and cooking places—the births for each perfon to be 6 feet by 18
inches, with the allowance of 56 gallons water and two
barrels bulk of ftowage for each perfon, befides fufficient
room to be left in the hold for provifions. Whatever
room remains in the veffel, to be at the difpofal of the
owner.

Eftimates to be given in to the fubfcriber; the loweft
only will be attended to.

ROBERT KALLEY.
Glaſgow, 5th. April, 1803.

Cost estimates invited from shippers for carrying 400 Skye people to
Prince Edward Island or Pictou. *From the* Glasgow Courier *9 April 1803.*

"Wanted a vessel to carry 400 passengers from Portree in Skye to
St. John or Pictou, Nova Scotia, to be ready for sea by 1st June. The
owner of the vessel to be at the expense of fitting up berths, furnishing water, casks and water with fuel and cooking places. The
berths for each person to be 6 ft by 18 inches, with the allowance
of 56 gallons water and 2 barrels bulk of stowage for each person
besides sufficient room to be left in the hold for provisions."[14]

Selkirk also sought advice from McKnight and McIlwraith, an Ayr-
shire firm which, by the early 1800s, had built up a considerable trade
with Quebec in timber, potash and grain. On their recommendation,
John MacDonald, a fellow-Scot, who "lives at Quebec during the sea-
son the river is open" became Lord Selkirk's shipping agent.[15] Mac-
Donald was responsible for dealing with the *Oughton*'s crew and cargo once she had completed her onward journey from Prince Edward
Island to Quebec. His instructions from McKnight and McIlwraith,
who actually owned the vessel, were to return to the Clyde with wheat

Posthumous portrait c. 1870, by Robert Harris of Dr. Angus MacAuley, Lord Selkirk's agent, who later became a speaker of the House of Assembly. *Courtesy PEI Public Archives and Records Office, 3733-11.*

if the price was favourable and to sell what he could from the outward journey:

"If wheat have come low, I will expect a quantity by the *Oughton* which vessel sailed eight days ago but may be two or three weeks detained as she carries out 200 passengers from South Uist to Charlottetown.... I desire you to sell every article on board of no use to the ship and which remained or might be laid in consequence of the emigrants— the camhouse [caboose] and empty puncheons are the most valuable, the former costing 18 guineas, the latter 13 s. each. Give the amount of the proceeds to Captain Baird to pay expenses of ship at Quebec and render me a particular slate of the sale. I suppose the store provisions will be taken by Lord Selkirk and paid for but if not, sell what is not useful for the crew."[16]

Captain Baird's instructions from the ship's owners for the return journey to Ayr left nothing to chance and tell us something of the perils posed by wartime conditions:

"I do not know exactly whether you will or not have a wheat cargo as I have limited Mr MacDonald who I do think will put some on board about my price, also nice oak, logs, spars, staves, beef, pork and oil. I trust with a cargo something like the above Mr MacDonald will give you dispatch [from Quebec] as I wish you to go a voyage during the winter—use your own direction coming home to avoid privateers and when you do sail use the utmost industry to make a quick voyage in which case, 10 to 1, you save me £350 insurance.... It is not improbable that the French may be in Ireland or Scotland by the time you arrive—it may be very proper you call at Lamlash or try to speak some outward bound vessel to learn the situation of the country at that time before you run into a harbour where there is danger or where they may be in force."[17]

The 800 or so who set sail on the *Dykes, Polly* and *Oughton* in June of 1803 all arrived safely in Orwell Bay during August without incident and within a few days of one another.[18] No actual passenger list survives but we have a partial list of the settlers who, some eight years later, signed a petition offering support to Angus MacAuley (Table 2).[19] We also know, from tombstone inscriptions and death notices, the names of around twenty-five emigrants from Skye and Wester Ross, who sailed on the *Polly* (Table 3). To Selkirk's annoyance, his ship, the *Dykes* arrived two days after the *Polly,* even though his was the first to leave. Anxious to have the settlement arrangements exactly as he wanted them, Selkirk immediately dispatched a message to Angus MacAuley, stating that the settlers were to be located in ten to twelve small villages rather than in the two to three larger villages which Dr. MacAuley was proposing. Selkirk's next immediate concern was to confront the people who were squatting on his land in lots 57 and 58 fearing that they would "gladly disgust the newcomers" in order to preserve their holdings. In fact, at the back of Selkirk's mind, throughout his first few weeks on the Island, was the constant worry that the many problems and frequent disillusionments of pioneer life would foster anti-emigration ammunition for the doom merchants back in Scotland or, worse still, would lead to a draining away of settlers from Belfast to North Carolina.

Meanwhile, Angus MacAuley was extremely disappointed to discover that while he had been chosen to recruit settlers, he had lost the plum job of managing Selkirk's business interests on the Island.[20] Although relations between MacAuley and Selkirk became irretrievably soured by this and other happenings, both remained popular with the original group of settlers.[21] Dr. MacAuley continued to preside

Table 3: Selkirk settlers who are commemorated in tombstone inscriptions or death notices as having sailed on the *Polly* in 1803*
*Source: PEI Genealogical Society, *From Scotland to Prince Edward Island*

Name Location	Yrs Born/Died	Scottish Origins	and Location	PEI Lot No
Beaton, Malcolm	1798 1877	Skye	Flat River	(60)
Campbell, Angus	1791 1888	West Isles	N/K	
Docherty, Donald	1789 1881	N/K		(50)
[Came with his parents]				
Furness, Ann	1786 1877	Skye (Kilmuir)		N/K
Gillis, Donald	1796 1874	N/K		N/K
MacAuly, Angus M D	1760 1827	N/K	Belfast	(58)
MacDonald, Donald R	1823 1891	N/K	Eldon	(57)
MacDonald, John	1802 1884	Skye	Orwell Cove	(57)
MacDonald, Margaret	1797 1881	N/K	Orwell	(50)
MacDougall, Donald	1789 1875	Skye	Belle Creek	(62)
MacEachern, Margaret	1792 1884	Inv'shire		(66)
MacLaren, Mrs John	1794 1881	N/K	Charlottetown	(33)
MacLean, Sarah	1796 1891	Mull		(16)
MacLeod, Malcolm	1746 1844	Skye	Pinette	(59)
MacLeod, Mary	1800 1892	N/K	Point Prim	(57)
MacRae, Finlay	1872	Applecross		N/K
MacRae, Margaret	1872	Applecross		N/K
Martin, Donald	1759 1848	Skye	Belfast	(58)
[Emigrated with Lord Selkirk. May have travelled on *Polly*.]				
Master, Margery	1798 1886	N/K	Vernon River	(49)
[Her father travelled on *'Polly'* in 1803.]				
Murchison, Mrs Alexander	1802 1894	Skye	Point Prim	(57)
[Travelled with her parents Mr & Mrs J. R. MacDonald.]				
Nicholson, Mary	1800 1886	N/K	Orwell Cove	(57)
Panting, Jane	1875	Inverness-shire	N/K	
Ross, Alexander	1798 1878	Skye	Wheatly River	(25)
[Came with his father. Buried in Lot 33.]				
Ross, Donald	1784 1866	Skye	Flat River	(60)
Stewart, Donald	1801 1887	Highlands	West River	(65)
[Came with his parents.]				

over the fledgling emigrant communities, acting as arbitrator when there were disputes, but Selkirk maintained a close eye on all settlement policy decisions.

Selkirk was adamant that success would only come if his settlers were totally self-reliant. Land could be purchased but not given free of charge. The same principle applied to provisioning. Selkirk employed an agent to purchase food and other supplies for his group until their farms became established, but settlers had to pay for such support. Those who could not pay were given assistance in the form of loans. Another important point of principle was the maintenance of strong community ties. Care was taken to ensure that the various settlements were within a reasonable distance of one another, that each contained self-supporting family groupings and that sufficient spaces were left in each settlement to allow for later settlement expansion.

> "It would be also desirable that the lots could be laid out somewhat wide of each other, so that the lands of different parties should have some intervals between them, which they could invite their friends to come after them and occupy...in taking several hundred acres, an individual does not imagine he shall cultivate or need it all himself, but he must have room to spread and room for his brother or his cousin that is to follow him."[22]

"On account of the probability of religion creating differences," Selkirk was convinced that the Skye and South Uist settlers should be kept well apart. His real concern was that his staunchly Presbyterian Skye settlers would react badly to having Catholics from South Uist as near neighbours. Anti-Catholic feelings on the Island were very strong and as Selkirk observed, the already-established Highland Catholics "are no favourites."[23] Dr. MacAuley expressed similar sentiments, but somewhat more colourfully:

> "the bulk of the inhabitants of the Island consisted of entrapped Loyalists and illiterate Roman Catholic Highlanders, the latter float-

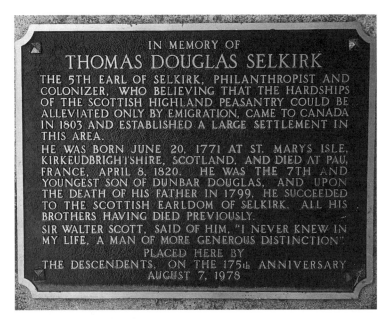

IN MEMORY OF
THOMAS DOUGLAS SELKIRK
THE 5TH EARL OF SELKIRK, PHILANTHROPIST AND
COLONIZER, WHO BELIEVING THAT THE HARDSHIPS
OF THE SCOTTISH HIGHLAND PEASANTRY COULD BE
ALLEVIATED ONLY BY EMIGRATION, CAME TO CANADA
IN 1803 AND ESTABLISHED A LARGE SETTLEMENT IN
THIS AREA.
HE WAS BORN JUNE 20, 1771 AT ST. MARYS ISLE,
KIRKEUDBRIGHTSHIRE, SCOTLAND, AND DIED AT PAU,
FRANCE, APRIL 8, 1820. HE WAS THE 7TH AND
YOUNGEST SON OF DUNBAR DOUGLAS, AND UPON
THE DEATH OF HIS FATHER IN 1799, HE SUCCEEDED
TO THE SCOTTISH EARLDOM OF SELKIRK, ALL HIS
BROTHERS HAVING DIED PREVIOUSLY.
SIR WALTER SCOTT, SAID OF HIM, "I NEVER KNEW IN
MY LIFE, A MAN OF MORE GENEROUS DISTINCTION".
PLACED HERE BY
THE DESCENDENTS, ON THE 175th ANNIVERSARY
AUGUST 7, 1978

Memorial plaque to Lord Selkirk. *Courtesy of PEI Public Archives and Records Office, Charlottetown Camera Club Collection, Acc. 2320/3–13.*

ing over the face of the country like *Scthyians* without money, *bed-cloaths*, or permanent holdings for residence."[24]

Selkirk initially tried to persuade the Uist contingent to take up land in lot 10, a remote and sparsely populated area on the northwest side of the Island. He knew perfectly well that the main concentration of Catholic Scots was in Kings County on the east of the Island. Predictably, the Uist settlers were outraged. Selkirk may not have realised that he was dealing with shrewd negotiators who knew that they had the backing of the highly influential Father Angus MacEachern. Acting as a mediator, Father MacEachern managed to persuade all parties that the Uist contingent should settle in lot 53, where they would be close to other Catholic Highland communities.[25] Selkirk also met with some resistance from a number of MacRae families, the "strong party of Ross-shire people," who having laid claim to "a choice situation in Point Prim," refused to take up the land he intended them to

Memorial to the Scottish emigrants who arrived with Lord Selkirk at Belfast in 1803. *Photograph by I.G. Campey.*

have. The MacRae's won out by simply refusing to budge and at least six of the original families, who mostly originated from Applecross, in Wester Ross, ended their days in the Point Prim area (lots 57 and 58).[26]

Unlike most emigrants who had to accept leaseholds, Selkirk encouraged his group to buy land. However, because of insufficient prior planning, settlers experienced a delay of three to four weeks while the necessary laying out of lots was agreed. The delay was a major hitch to this otherwise smooth operation. Emigrants started to doubt the viability of the venture and were even sceptical about buying Selkirk's land even though it was "offered at very low rates, scarcely amounting to one-half of the price usually demanded by other proprietors of the Island."[27] But, in spite of this early set-back, the settlers eventually took up their lots, sold as fifty to one hundred acre holdings, and as Selkirk observed:

"It was not till they dispersed to their separate lots, till by working upon them they had begun to form a local attachment, and to view their property with a sort of paternal fondness that I could reckon the settlement as fairly begun."[28]

They wasted no time in building their houses, which were "constructed without any other materials than what the forests afford, and without the aid of any tool but the axe" and soon had the basics of life. As Selkirk had predicted, they quickly demonstrated their natural aptitude for pioneer life having:

"a great advantage over people who are accustomed to better accommodation, and who would have employed a great proportion of their time in building comfortable houses. They [Highlanders], on the contrary, had soon secured themselves a shelter, poor indeed in appearance, and of narrow dimensions, but such as they could put up with for a temporary resource; and immediately applied themselves with vigour to the essential object of clearing their lands. They proceeded in this with assiduity; and though the work was of a nature so totally new to them, they had made a considerable progress in cutting down the trees before the winter set in. The same work was continued during winter, whenever the weather was not too severe and upon the opening of spring, the land was finally prepared for the seed."[29]

In all, Selkirk acquired 143,000 acres of land on the Island from individual proprietors but directed most of his energy towards the 80,000 acres within the Belfast area.[30] By 1807 he had sold around 16,000 acres to over 150 individuals. His policy of selling rather than leasing land encouraged population growth and quickly transformed

Early photograph of St. John's Presbyterian Church at Belfast.
Courtesy of PEI Public Archives and Records Office, Acc. 4390/7.

the chosen sites into flourishing settlements. Scots eventually dominated the southeast side of the Island, particularly lots 50, 57, 58, 59, 60, 62 and 63. Most originated from Skye, and to a lesser extent Wester Ross, the two areas from which the original 1803 exodus had originated. Selkirk's decision in 1803 to settle the Roman Catholics from South Uist in Kings County achieved his desired outcome of dividing settlers by religion. By 1848 there were large concentrations of Presbyterians

Picnic celebration in 1903 to mark the 100th anniversary of the arrival of the Selkirk settlers at Belfast. *Courtesy of PEI Public Archives and Records Office Acc., 3423/1.*

from Skye and Wester Ross in lots 57, 58, 60 and 62 and very few Roman Catholics of Scottish descent.[31] The opposite was the case in Kings County. Nearly all emigration from South Uist and other Catholic areas of the Western Isles was concentrated in this one County, and here Presbyterian Scots were a rarity.[32] By 1824, Belfast acquired St. John's Presbyterian Church, a large and beautifully-built church which was erected on land that had been originally granted by Selkirk.[33] Belfast's success was noted in evidence to the *1826 Emigration Select Committee* and by 1828, its population had quadrupled:

> "...he [Selkirk] brought his colony from the Highlands and Isles of Scotland and by the convenience of the tenures under which he gave the land and by persevering industry on their part...the inhabitants are all in easy circumstances and their numbers have increased from 800 to nearly 3,000."[34]

Selkirk's 1803 venture was the last great emigration scheme undertaken from Scotland under the auspices of a proprietor. The growth in the North American timber trade in the early 1800s revolutionized the cost of transatlantic transport. This meant that, instead of having to rely on benefactors with money to charter a ship, ordinary emigrants could simply purchase places on any of the ships which made regular Atlantic crossings. In 1806, when Britain was at war with France and sea crossings were at their most perilous, seven ships, each with large numbers of emigrants arrived at Prince Edward Island. This marked the beginning of the new age in emigrant shipping where individuals, working through shipping agents, purchased places on ships of their choice to those destinations where shippers sought their timber supplies. It was a complex trade which opened up new shipping routes between Scotland and the eastern Maritimes and completely transformed emigrant transport and settlement opportunities. As we shall see in the following chapter, Prince Edward Island's pulling power during the Napoleonic War years was particularly impressive. The catalyst and ongoing propellent was the North American timber trade.

IV

THE COMING OF THE TIMBER TRADE

"He little dreamed, as he often told me that, when he was carrying
on his back 15 or 20 miles a single bushel of potatoes around the
margin of the shore, he should live to see the day when he would be
able to drive in his carriage from one end of the Island to the other."[1]

THESE WORDS WERE attributed, in 1851, to the father of James
McCallum, one of the first British settlers to arrive in Brackley Point
(lot 33), and a prime example of the "worthy and industrious race of
men, chiefly from Scotland" who gave the settlement its "neat, clean,
well-built farm houses with large barns and convenient outbuildings."[2] James McCallum's father had almost certainly been a member
of one of the proprietor-led groups which came to the Island in the
late eighteenth century. He would have come to Prince Edward Island
at a time when the area was beginning to attract Clyde shippers who
were seeking new sources of timber.[3] The sudden explosion in the timber trade, from the early 1800s, revolutionised shipping services and
made transatlantic travel affordable to the average emigrant. The
dawning of mass transport created the conditions necessary for population growth and prosperity. The timber trade and the transport
opportunities it provided gave Brackley Point, and many places like
it, its new generations of Scottish emigrants and gave older settlers,
like James McCallum's father, their affluent lifestyle.

Homestead of Neil McCallum and family at Brackley Point in lot 33. Engraving published in Meacham's *Historical Atlas,* 1880. This exemplifies the "neat, clean well-built farm houses with large barns and convenient outbuildings" which John Lawson attributed to "the race of men, chiefly from Scotland" in his *Letters on Prince Edward Island* published 1851.

The rush for North American timber had its roots in the Napoleonic Wars. The blockade of 1806, which effectively barred British ships from the Baltic, forced timber merchants to look to Quebec and the Maritimes for their supplies. Before this happened, British merchants had relied almost entirely on the Baltic as a source of wood. Even when the Baltic was re-opened, the government encouraged the fledgling North American timber trade by making Baltic timber subject to duties. This was done both to guarantee supplies and to support the then struggling colonial economies. Tariffs were first introduced in 1811 and had the effect of pricing Baltic timber out of the market. The greater distance to North America ceased to be an obstacle to profitable trade and Britain's timber purchases were effectively transferred from the Baltic to North America. In 1807, Prince Edward Island exported 1,000 loads of timber to Britain. By 1819, it exported over 17,000 loads.[4]

By 1820 timber exports had become the bedrock of the Island's economy. Timber gave the Island most of its revenue as well as much needed employment opportunities during winter months. The timber trade actually financed four-fifths of the costs of the Island's imports

LANDS.

TO BE SOLD
BY PUBLIC AUCTION,
At the Court-House,

Charlotte-Town, at One o'clock, on Wednes-
day the 29th day of June next,

4800 acres

part of Lot or Township No. 8,
fronting on Wolf-Inlet, the division lines of
which have been ascertained. The soil of the
above property is excellent, a deep black
loam, and well Timbered; there is a considerable quantity of Pine Timber fit for exportation, and also a quantity of Cedar. The
Marshes in front which are very extensive,
will cut at the lowest calculation, from 40 to
50 tons of Hay, of a superior quality; there
is also a Sand-hill, which forms the one side
of Wolf Inlet, on which may be cut upwards of
40 tons of Hay. There are three fine fresh
water Rivers running through the property,
two of which abound with very fine trout:
great quantities of herring annually frequent
Wolf-Inlet in the Spring, and cod fish are
caught in great plenty very convenient.

Also, on the same day,

2500 acres

part of Lot or Township No. 52,
being No. 8 by the division lines of the Lot, on
which are great quantities of Pine and Hardwood Timber fit for exportation. The plan of
the above property may be seen; and further
particulars made known by reference to the
Proprietor Andrew M'Donald, Esq. at Three
Rivers, or to Mr. Donald M'Donald, Merchant, Charlotte-Town.

Andrew M'Donald.

March 14.

Notice of 4,800 acres of land "with considerable quantity of pine timber" to be sold by Public Auction in Charlottetown. The owner is the Scottish-born Andrew MacDonald, who was a prominent storekeeper in the Three Rivers area. *From* Prince Edward Island Register, *15 November 1825.*

from Britain.⁵ As was to be found throughout British America, Scots were quick to realise the profits to be had from the timber trade in the eastern Maritimes and in the rapidly-developing shipbuilding indus-tries which followed on its heels. Appropriately, it was at a St. Andrew's Day dinner in Charlottetown, in 1825, that glasses were raised to prosperity in shipbuilding:

> "By means of it [shipbuilding], our exports considerably exceeded our imports in amount, and a great part of the balance which remained went to reward the ingenuity and recompense the manu-al labour of the country."⁶

Right from the start, the timber trade left shippers with a huge amount of spare shipping capacity to fill on their westward journeys. Shipowners, with empty holds to fill, were happy to have emigrants who benefited from relatively low fares. Many offered a total package of both transport and land. In 1811, Angus Campbell, a Stornoway shipowner, was preparing to take emigrants on his outward journey to the Island to collect timber, saying that he had "great tracts of land… and will sell them reasonably to settlers on their arrival." This was wartime, so he had also to give additional reassurances:

> "The *James* (350 tons)…to sail from Stornoway to Prince Edward Island…master well-armed now fitting out at Rodel in Harris…ship returns immediately back with a cargo of timber…passengers wishing to settle in Prince Edward Island cannot have a better opportunity."⁷

The *James'* arrival in Stornoway appears to have been the result of an approach made by John MacKenzie, another Stornoway shipper to a Liverpool colleague:

> "You are within time of sending ships for timber to Prince Edward Island and to the neighbourhood of Pictou…. I have nearly 150 pas-sengers engaged to furnish them a ship for the Spring say, 1811….

The cause of my writing you is to know if you would come under engagement to send a ship for them here…to remain here for 10 to 15 days…ship to furnish provisions, water, doctor, berths for the voyage, to pay all Customs charges and to ship on board any little luggage each passenger would have…I beg to know the lowest freight you would take for each full grown passenger above 2 years male or female, for each passenger less than 12 years of age, not exceeding to two years, the rest to go *gratis* but to incur no provisions *but* water from the ship."[8]

The greater security risks of travelling in wartime conditions must have deterred emigration, but it clearly had not halted it. Some 1,200 Highlanders entered the Maritime ports of Charlottetown and Pictou between 1805 and 1815, having boarded ship at either Oban, Stornoway, Tobermory, Thurso or Fort William.[9] During this same period, six ships took emigrants from Stromness and Stornoway to Hudson's Bay. The opponents of emigration were appalled by these events and mounted strenuous campaigns to curtail the rising tide of emigration from the Highlands. Selkirk's settlers were accused of scurrilously selling their land holdings to fellow Highlanders at a profit.[10] But "one person of the name of Robertson" of Prince Edward Island was the prime scoundrel. With his involvement in the Island's timber trade and his wide-ranging contacts in the Highlands, James Robertson had considerable success in getting emigrants to sail on his ships to the Island. News of his success even got to London where newspapers reported on the "poor ignorant wretches" who had been deluded by false promises and paid exorbitant fares.[11]

In spite of the best efforts of the anti-emigration propagandists, the exceptionally high fares, and the wars raging between Britain and France, Highlanders made their way to the Island in ever increasing numbers. At least 600 Highlanders came to the Island in 1806—making it a bumper year. In 1805 there had been just two ships—the *Nancy,* sailing from Tobermory, and the *Northern Friends of Clyde* from Stornoway, together taking around 120 emigrants to the Island. But, in 1806, there were four ships which left from Tobermory: the *Rambler* of Leith, the *Humphreys* of London, the *Isle of Skye* of Aberdeen and the *Rebecca and Sarah* of Leith (carrying between them around 400 passengers), one from Oban—the *Spencer* of Newcastle (with just over 100 passengers), one from Thurso—the *Elizabeth and Ann* of Newcastle (with similar numbers) and the *Pallas* from Greenock with unknown numbers. Two years later the *Elizabeth,* the *Mars,* and the *Clarendon* of Hull took some 400 passengers to the Island from Oban and further, unknown numbers, followed them, in 1810, sailing on the *Catherine* of Leith and the *Phoenix.*[12]

These ships attracted far more interest and paperwork than was usually the case. They even merited that rarest form of ship documentation—passenger lists, which survive for the 1806 crossings of the *Rambler* of Leith, the *Humphreys* of London, the *Isle of Skye* of Aberdeen, the *Spencer* of Newcastle, and the *Elizabeth and Ann* of Newcastle and for the 1808 crossing of the *Clarendon* of Hull (Appendix 1).[13] The 1803 Passenger Act had created new regulations for shippers which, although ostensibly intended to ensure adequate food and space for passengers, had the effect of adding considerably to costs and overall bureaucracy.[14] The passenger lists of 1806, and their survival, are lasting reminders of the greater controls placed on passenger travel at the time. Emigrants undoubtedly paid much higher fares, but they got much more space. However, emigrants valued low fares far more than their creature comforts and, in the end, the government had to bow to pressure, which it did in 1816, to repeal the legislation, which was generally thought to be impractical and unnecessarily burdensome.[15]

James Robertson was an articulate man who, like Selkirk, understood Highlander grievances. When the *Inverness Journal* claimed that he caused impressionable Highlanders to imagine "a lairdship and an air-built castle of his own in Prince Edward Island," he countered by saying that he took particular pleasure in alleviating the suffering of so many people "from that abject servility in which they were maintained on several Highland estates" and continued:

"I have the pleasing reflection of...having prevented their going to the American States and of having furnished them with the means of getting to a British settlement, where, if they are industrious, for idleness meets with no reward, they shall become their own masters, and not be considered slaves of other men, not born to toil under humiliating and rigourous privations."[16]

If we take press and other reports at face value we would conclude that James Robertson was an utter rogue. But much of the criticism levelled at him was bogus. High fares were a fact of life at the time and all shippers complained bitterly about the impact of the 1803 Act which did dramatically raise fares.[17] While his critics from Blair Atholl claimed, in 1808, that he "has lately carried off about 700 whom he agrees to transport to Prince Edward Island at a rate of £9 a piece, upon which he will make a profit of £5 a head independent of the profit on the sale of land or by the bondage to which some of them engage themselves," Robertson maintained that he had offered reasonable terms.[18] But the telling point about Robertson was his success in attracting so many emigrants. They were not being forced to use his services but were doing so in spite of much anti-emigration publicity and Robertson's seemingly bad reputation. A possible clue, as to his selling technique, comes from his appearance in the *Clarendon*'s passenger list completed before she sailed from Oban in 1808. What better reassurance to offer nervous and sceptical emigrants than to travel with them from Scotland as James Robertson, Junior of Queens County, Prince Edward Island (Appendix I).

The trade grew so quickly and chaotically in Prince Edward Island in 1817 to 1818 that settlers and ship masters were often caught trying to barter timber and goods with each other, privately, in flagrant breach of the Customs regulations. There were complaints that merchants like Donald MacDonald of Three Rivers, regularly evaded customs procedures, when he shipped his timber cargoes out every year.[19] In fact, until enforceable regulations came into effect, the mere fact that timber could be loaded from countless locations along coastlines, anywhere in the Maritimes, meant that settlers, ship masters and spec-ulative merchants were more or less free to make informal deals over timber when it suited them.

By the turn of the nineteenth century, Scottish settlers had estab-lished footholds at Malpeque Bay, Stanhope, Scotchfort and Belfast. These had all been group settlements, led and organised by well-resourced Scottish proprietors. But with the steady growth in the east-ern Maritime timber trade from 1806, emigration was no longer restricted to large proprietor-led groups who could fill a ship. The advent of regular and affordable transatlantic shipping opened up emigration as a realistic prospect to people of average means. All they needed was their fare and information on the next available ship, both of which were ascertained and negotiated through agents, working on behalf of the shippers who were touting for business. The result was a sustained influx of Scots, during the first two decades of the nine-teenth century. As we might expect, some joined fellow Scots in the older communities, such as those in Malpeque, Belfast and Scotchfort. But these settlements also provided the launch-pad for considerable expansion into neighbouring townships. By the early 1820s, when Irish immigration to the Island was just starting its explosive rise, the Scottish domination of the east side of the island was already a *fait accompli,* and was also evident in the string of townships stretching from Malpeque Bay to New Argyle.

Throughout this period, the Scottish occupation of territory appears to have reflected more than just a desire to build on earlier settlement footholds. The large contingents from the Argyll Islands of Colonsay and Mull, who arrived during the great emigration wave of 1806 to 1810, strode out into new areas, which at the time were almost devoid of settlers. Malpeque, which might have been expected to be their first choice, was completely by-passed. After 1806, Malpeque was not even attracting much interest from Kintyre, the area in Argyll, from which its first settlers had originated. Malpeque may have just run out of suitable new land. But the fact that these emigrants chose the western approaches to Hillsborough Bay, the Island's largest tim-

Homestead of Lauchlan McMillan at Covehead West in Lot 33. Engraving published 1880 in Meacham's *Historical Atlas*.

ber port, as their favoured spot, suggests that they were motivated, at least to some extent, by economic considerations.

Country storekeepers played a key role in co-ordinating the activities of the many settlers who were engaged in some aspect of timber cutting or transport. Working closely with local merchants, they provided settlers with credit and took their produce, which often included cut wood, as repayment. Together the merchants, storekeepers, brokers and sawmillers formed an intricate commercial framework along with the farmer/lumberers who actually cut the trees.[20] As Lord Selkirk observed during his 1803 visit to Pictou:

> "The lumber is mostly contracted for with settlers in return for stores furnished them and delivered at the wharfs—each storekeeper has his wharf where the logs are kept by a floating Boom confined in a Bay ready to put on board the ships."[21]

The port at Georgetown was the second-most important timber port on the Island, after Charlottetown.[22] This may have been the deciding factor which led so many Highlanders to settle in or close to

Homestead of Alexander McBeath and family at Lot 34. Engraving published 1880 in Meacham's *Historical Atlas*.

the Three Rivers area (lots 51 to 53). Another factor may have been the business acumen of one man—Andrew MacDonald. Shortly after his arrival from Scotland he purchased all of Panmure Island (lot 61) lying just to the south of Georgetown, and established a general store, which became the centre of business activity within the Three Rivers area.[23] He had left Arisaig (Inverness-shire) in 1806 and travelled to the Island on the *Isle of Skye* of Aberdeen in 1806. He evidently had planned right from the beginning to become a storekeeper since he arrived with more than the normal amount of personal luggage. He came with large quantities of: general equipment, clothing, household goods, shoes, furniture, horse equipment, farming items, cloth, cutlery and handkerchiefs.[24] Little is known of his early business dealings; but given the clannish tendency of most Scottish entrepreneurs, the likelihood is that any capital he brought with him only benefited fellow Scots. We get some indication of his sizeable land holdings from his 1825 newspaper advertisement which showed him trying to sell 4,800 acres in lot 8 and 2,500 acres in lot 52, with a prime feature of the land being its "pine and hardwood timber fit for exportation."[25]

Most of the Scots who came to the Three Rivers area originated from the Highlands and Islands, although few came from Andrew MacDonald's native Arisaig. There was a particularly sizeable influx from Perthshire to lot 52, many originating from the Blair Atholl estate:

Green Hill' farm residence of Donald McDougald and family at Canoe Cove in Lot 65. Gravestone inscriptions show that he originated from Mull while his wife, Margaret Shaw, came from the Island of Jura. Engraving published 1880 in Meacham's *Historical Atlas*. Note the "design for the new house" in the top right hand corner.

"The emigration from this part of the country [Blair Atholl] to Prince Edward Island has been pretty considerable of late and does not appear to have been the consequence of any change of system toward the tenants as the Duke continues to let the small farms. But people have been going about the county holding out such golden prospects that the poor people cannot resist the temptation."[26]

This was 1808 and no wonder that alarm bells were being raised on the Blair Atholl estate. Tenants were leaving in droves for Prince Edward Island. James Robertson's ships took them to the Island and, in spite of a concerted campaign against him and the other emigration agents active in Perthshire, the exodus seemed unstoppable. The prospect of re-establishing a Perthshire community on land which they would eventually hope to own was indeed "a golden prospect," worth striving for. They founded New Perth in 1809 (lot 52) and it continued to attract Perthshire settlers over the next ten years but numbers declined thereafter.[27]

FIGURE 3   PREDOMINANT AREAS OF SCOTLAND FROM WHICH
P.E.I.'S SCOTTISH SETTLERS ORIGINATED, 1770–1850

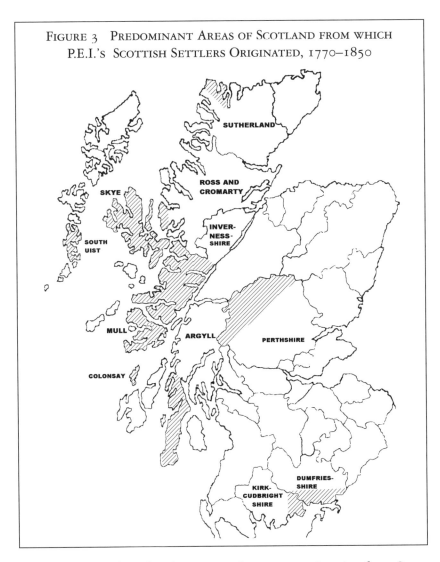

Late eighteenth and early nineteenth century emigration from Scotland to Prince Edward Island was essentially a pull from the west (Figure 3). Ships on their way to British America for timber could conveniently call for passengers at ports in the west, thus creating a markedly improved service for emigrants living in or near coastal areas on the west of the country.[28] The primary exodus came from the Western Isles, especially Skye, Mull and Colonsay, but mainland Scotland also lost people to the Island. Emigration from Sutherland and Wester Ross, which only began in the early 1800s, was highly focussed around two specific areas. Large clusters came from Durness in Sutherland and Applecross in Wester Ross and in each case they claimed their own part of the Island (Figure 4). Lots 20 and 21 received their first group from Durness in 1806, people who would have sailed on the *Elizabeth and Ann* from Thurso that year. Established from 1773, the New London and Granville areas, in which they settled, also had long-standing associations with "Lowland Scotch," who were described by an 1851 commentator as "an industrious and thriving race."[29] But it was the Sutherlanders who forged the strongest allegiance to the area which survived for over 40 years.[30] Extended families of MacKays formed the backbone of this exodus. William MacKay took up land at lot 21 in 1806, and he was followed to the same lot by Hugh and Donald Mackay, who arrived in 1815, then by Robert and Hector MacKay who arrived in 1835 and finally by William MacKay who came in 1841.

Ross-shire emigrants had first been attracted to the Island in 1803, coming as members of the Selkirk expedition. As might be expected, most settled in the Selkirk holdings at Belfast (lots 57, 58, 60 and 62). But it was the steady stream of emigrants from Applecross which particularly stands out. The Belfast townships received a regular intake from this part of Wester Ross for some 30 years. Two lots, lots 58 (Belfast) and 60 (Flat River), appeared to separate two prominent Applecross families—the MacKenzies and MacRaes. The MacRaes generally favoured lot 58 and the MacKenzies, lot 60. In 1811, a group of MacRaes and MacKenzies from Applecross extended their pioneering efforts beyond Prince Edward Island by establishing a small settlement in the Middle River area of Cape Breton.[31]

It must be remembered that the Sutherland and Wester Ross exodus to the Island was only a tiny part of the whole story. It was Nova Scotia (particularly Pictou), and not the Island, which found most favour with Sutherland and Ross-shire emigrants and had done so, from the late eighteenth century. The ones who chose the Island were

FIGURE 4 CONCENTRATION OF SCOTTISH-BORN
HOUSEHOLDERS IN PEI TOWNSHIPS

When?

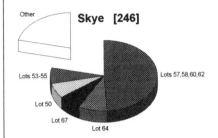

Skye [246]

Other

Lots 53-55

Lot 50

Lot 67

Lot 64

Lots 57,58,60,62

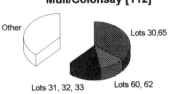

Mull/Colonsay [112]

Other

Lots 30,65

Lots 31, 32, 33

Lots 60, 62

Dumfrieshire [80]

Lots 28-29

Other

Lots 17,19,25,26

Perthshire [69]

Lots 33,34

Other

Lot 47

Lots 52-54

Ross-shire [60]

Other

Lots 57,58,60,62

Sutherland [41]

Other

Lots 20-21

The number in square brackets refers to the number of householders

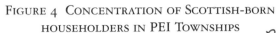
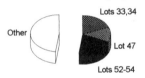

therefore very much the exception. Similarly, having attracted so many emigrants from west Inverness-shire in the 1770s, and again in the 1790s, the Island experienced little follow-on emigration, although huge numbers from this part of Scotland went off to colonise Upper Canada and other regions of the Maritimes.[32]

Emigration from Perthshire to the Island lasted longer and was focussed on three distinct areas (Figure 4). Their earliest footholds were at Stanhope (lot 34) and Beaton Point (lot 47), which were settled in the early 1770s, and some forty years later yet another site was established at New Perth (lot 52).[33] However, these pioneering efforts were relatively short-lived. With its better climate and soil fertility, Upper Canada soon beckoned. The turning point occurred in 1815. The lure of government-funded passages, a one-off scheme offered that year to encourage Scots to settle in the Rideau valley military settlements in Upper Canada, drew large numbers from Perthshire, particularly from the Breadalbane estate.[34]

Three years later, a group of 300 from the Breadalbane estate (from Dull, Killin, Comrie and Balquhidder) left for Upper Canada. However, not everyone was content with this decision. A few had second thoughts. After arriving in Montreal, they immediately got on a ship to Cape Breton.[35] Apparently because of dense fog, their captain lost his way, and their ship landed at Prince Edward Island by mistake. Arriving "in a deplorable state of poverty," they are thought to have settled at lots 26 and 27 in Seven Mile Bay (Table 4).[36] Given that the adjoining lot 67 contains a place called Breadalbane, the likelihood is that they did settle in this area, although no traces of this group survive. Breadalbane eventually became a major Scottish preserve, but not until 1830 and as a result of an influx from Skye, not from Perthshire.

Large numbers of Renfrewshire and Lanarkshire people had also responded to the government's offer of free passages to Upper Canada but, as was the case with Perthshire emigrants, a small number opted for Prince Edward Island instead. A group, mainly from Renfrewshire came to the Island in 1818 but, having established the New Glasgow settlement (lot 23) at Rustico Bay, their venture fizzled out. Once again

Table 4: Perthshire emigrants who relocated themselves in PEI by 1820 [PRO CO 226/36]

[The passengers listed below had sailed from Greenock for Quebec on either the *Curlew* or *Jane* in 1818, but they later relocated themselves in PEI. They represented only a small fraction of the large contingent of tenants from the Breadalbane estate who chose PEI in preference to Upper Canada. Some 205 sailed to Quebec on the *Curlew*, 106 in the *Sophia* of Ayr and an unknown number on the *Jane* of Sunderland. Passenger lists survive for the *Curlew* and *Sophia* but not for the *Jane* (see PRO CO 384/3 pp. 123–27).

The small group who relocated in PEI petitioned the Colonial Office for help in 1820, claiming that they were in a most deplorable state of poverty].

Curlew Passengers (all originated from Dull parish)

John Stewart
Elizabeth Stewart wife

John Kenady
Christy Kenady wife
Mary Kenady
James Kenady

Duncan Cameron
Margaret Cameron wife
Isabel Cameron
Daniel Cameron

Finley Cameron
Jannet Cameron wife

Hugh McDearmed
Jannet McDearmed wife
Margaret McDearmed
Janet McDearmed

Jane of Sunderland Passengers*

James Stewart	Peter McVain
John Stewart	Grace McVain
Margaret Stewart	Alexander McVain
Alexander Stewart	David McVain
Elizabeth Stewart	Margaret McVain
David Stewart	James McVain

William Stewart	Jannet McVain
Isabel Stewart	Grace McVain
Jannet Stewart	John McVain
	William McVain

*Because no passenger list survives for the *Jane,* the Perthshire origins of this small group is not known. The *Curlew* passenger list reveals that most originated from Dull, Killin and Comrie while most of the passengers who sailed on the *Sophia* originated from Balquihidder and Kincardine.

competition from Upper Canada robbed the Island of Scottish settlers.

But there were parts of Scotland which maintained long-standing links with the Island—none more so than the Western Isles. Belfast continued to attract Skye settlers during the first two decades of the nineteenth century, although not in large numbers. The further reinforcements who came in the late 1820s, and again in the early 1840s, extended Scottish-held territory within the Belfast area into lots 50 and 64, while opening up a new foothold at lot 67 (Figure 4).[37] Colonsay and Mull emigrants, who first came in the early 1800s, settled mainly in Argyle Shore (lot 30) and New Argyle (lot 65), with some also taking up land in adjoining areas, as well as in the Belfast townships (lots 60 and 62). The likelihood is that the land was taken by squatting. They chose well. This was an area in which newly-arrived emigrants would have been particularly well placed to benefit from the Island's improving trade and economic opportunities. The fact that they were no real distance from Charlottetown, the place where they disembarked from their ships, must also have appealed, since this reduced both the cost and strain of the overall journey. The Mull and Colonsay attachment to these areas lingered for some 30 years. As before, emigration was characterised by large surges of people who entered the Island in two waves—one occurring in 1816–1821 and another in 1829–1833.[38]

After the Napoleonic Wars, the Island won few adherents from mainland Scotland except, that is, for Dumfriesshire which was the one exception. Dumfries developed trading links with British America much later than the Clyde, where Atlantic shipping routes had been established from the late 1790s. These Dumfries' links were initially mainly confined to Prince Edward Island and New Brunswick.[39] Thus, from 1816, Dumfriesshire emigrants had regular access to Prince Edward Island, but not Quebec. However good Upper Canada may have seemed, getting to it would have been cumbersome and expensive and, for about a decade, the Island experienced a steady influx from Dumfriesshire.

EMIGRANTS FROM DUMFRIESSHIRE

"No settlers are prized more…upon that Island from
Dumfriesshire and the southern counties of Scotland. None excel
them in agricultural knowledge, domestic economy or steady
industrious habits. None who can supply more of their own
wants with their own hands, submit without murmuring to mean
fare or make greater exertions to increase their own comforts.
I mean such of them as are sober and industrious; but I cannot say
they are all so. I would rank the Highlanders as next to these in
eligibility and the well-behaved Irish next, if not equal to them;
and the English as the most unsuitable of all."[1]

THESE WORDS WERE written by Walter Johnstone, a Dumfriesshire
man who took it upon himself to research Prince Edward Island and
produce an emigrant guide packed full of detailed information about
the Island's climate, soil quality, methods of agriculture and state of its
settlements. Having completed a grand tour of the Island in 1820–
1821, Johnstone recorded his observations and advice to emigrants as
a series of letters which he addressed to a fellow Dumfriesshire man,
Rev. John Wightman, who subsequently arranged for their publication.[2] Their availability was widely publicised in Dumfriesshire newspapers.[3] Not surprisingly, Johnstone gave Dumfriesshire settlers top
ranking. His lukewarm commendation of Highlanders and obvious

disapproval of the English typifies the ethnic tensions which were prevalent at the time, although such attitudes were usually more common in new arrivals, than in established settlers.

Johnstone recorded his observations some five years after emigration from the southwest Borders began its dramatic rise. It was not long before this exodus attracted the attention of the *Scots Magazine* who reported that in one week alone, in 1819, no less than 591 people had departed from the port of Dumfries for British America.[4] Johnstone was therefore, to some extent, preaching to the converted and responding to an increasing demand for knowledge about the Island and its prospects for ordinary settlers. Given that he was a well-known local figure, his optimistic accounts of the Island's agricultural and economic opportunities could well have tipped the balance for many:

"They export livestock of all kinds, grain and potatoes, to Newfoundland; grain, pork and potatoes to Miramichi, and grain and potatoes to Halifax.... The Islanders enjoy a privilege which many of the labouring classes at home cannot at present obtain; they may all be employed in cultivating the ground; and the ground, I have heard it said, is so very grateful that no man ever yet bestowed prudent labour upon it but it repaid him for his toil."[5]

Walter Johnstone's visits to the Island occurred shortly before the Presbyterian community in and near Charlottetown began raising funds to build a Church and acquire a minister "of the Established Church of Scotland."[6] This might explain his involvement with the "few Highland settlers" at Three Rivers and on lot 48 near Charlottetown who sought his help in obtaining "ministers of the Gospel, who can preach in Gaelic and English":

"We send this by the hands of Walter Johnstone, a native of Dumfriesshire, who has been occasionally visiting us these sixteen months past. We can bear the most ample testimony of his Christian conduct, and great exertions to erect Sabbath Schools all over

In the Press, and speedily will be published,
Price to Subscribers, 1s.
A SERIES OF LETTERS,
DESCRIPTIVE OF
PRINCE EDWARD ISLAND,
IN THE
GULPH OF ST LAWRENCE;
ADDRESSED
TO THE REV. JOHN WIGHTMAN,
MINISTER OF KIRKMAHOE,
DUMFRIES-SHIRE.
BY WALTER JOHNSTONE,
A native of the same County.

The Author of these Letters went out for the express pur-
pose of surveying Prince Edward Island, and collecting information on the subject of Emigration.   During two Sum-
mers, and one Winter, he was assiduously engaged in the
prosecution of this object; and the small volume now pre-
sented to the Public, will be found to contain a full and
particular account of the Climate, Soil, Natural Productions,
and Mode of Husbandry adopted in the Island; together
with Sketches of Scenery, Manners of the Inhabitants, &c.
&c.; the whole being intended for the guidance of future
Emigrants, particularly as to what Implements and Necessaries it may be proper to provide themselves with before
crossing the Atlantic.

Subscriptions will be received by the Dumfries-shire and
Galloway Booksellers, &c. and by the Author at his house,
No. 53, Glasgow-street, Maxwelltown.

Advertisement for Walter Johnstone's series of published letters on Prince Edward Island. *From* Dumfries
and Galloway Courier, *12 March 1822.*

the Island, wherever proper teachers can be found to carry them on
afterwards. By his instrumentality one was instituted here, which
has prospered beyond our highest expectations. He is now about to
return to his family at Dumfries; it is therefore our prayer to the
Father of mercies that he may be carried home in safety and that
many such may come to visit or reside amongst us."[7]

While Walter Johnstone undoubtedly stimulated the Dumfriesshire
exodus to Prince Edward Island in his time, emigration from this area
had actually begun in the late eighteenth century. The first contingents
to arrive on the Island with settlers from Dumfriesshire, Kirkcudbrightshire and Wigtownshire came in two separate sailings of the
Lovelly Nelly in 1774 and 1775.[8] Substantial numbers also left at this
time for New York and other unknown destinations in the southern

Dumfries from the New Bridge. Engraving by John Gellatly and drawing by A.S. Masson c. 1830. *Courtesy of Dumfries and Galloway Libraries, Information and Archives.*

colonies. The timing of these early arrivals to the Island could not have been worse. Coming at a time when the American War of Independence was getting underway, their hopes of establishing viable settlements were slim at best. Nothing tangible survives of their presence on the Island, although the favoured sites of later Dumfriesshire arrivals make us suspect that Dumfriesshire's associations with the Island date back to the eighteenth century.

While there were these excursions of the mid-1770s, people in the southwest Borders had to wait for some 40 years before regular shipping services to British America became available. Unlike the Clyde which sustained American trade links during the late eighteenth and early nineteenth centuries, the port of Dumfries did little British American trade until after 1816. Thus the combination of a post-war economic slump and the availability of regular transatlantic transport created the conditions necessary for a marked and short-lived exodus of people from the southwest Borders to the Maritimes. It began with a flourish from 1816 to 1822, then slowly petered out.

Until the mid-1820s nearly all emigration from the area was directed at the Maritimes. The reason is hardly surprising. Because Dumfries' principal trading links were initially with New Brunswick, and to a lesser extent Prince Edward Island, the cheapest, most frequent and direct shipping routes open to people were to the eastern Maritimes. There are no official figures, so numbers must be approximated from newspaper reports and customs records. These sources suggest that at least 3,000 people sailed to the Maritimes from 1816 to 1821 and most were destined for New Brunswick (Table 5).[9] Prince Edward Island got few of these emigrants until 1819. The peak years were 1820 to 1821, but the actual numbers to arrive on the Island can not be accurately quantified since only aggregate figures, which include New Brunswick-bound passengers, are available.[10] Official figures tell us of a further, but less pronounced surge in passenger numbers between 1829 and 1834, another period of economic depression, when around 1,400 emigrants set sail from Dumfries for British America. But, by this time Dumfries was doing regular trade with Quebec, and Upper Canada, not the Maritimes, was the favoured destination of most emigrants from the southwest Borders.[11]

Unlike most emigrants from the Highlands and Islands, Dumfriesshire emigrants did not dominate particular areas of the Island. They were widely dispersed over a number of townships (Figure 4). What particularly characterizes them was their tendency to seek out sites in, or close to, Loyalist settlements.[12] In other words, Dumfriesshire emigrants were drawn primarily to places which had their antecedents in the late eighteenth century. In the emigration surges after 1816, they chose Loyalist strongholds like Bedeque (lots 25 and 26) and were even more readily drawn to sites to the east of Bedeque, the so-called "beautiful settlement of Tryon" (lots 28 and 29), which in 1839 boasted a population of 1,100.[13] They were also to be found within the Isthmus between Bedeque and Malpeque Bay (especially at lots 17 and 19), another strongly Loyalist area. We therefore have to consider the possibility that it was Loyalists, originating from the southwest of Scotland, who gave these areas their particular appeal to later Dumfriesshire emigrants.

The earliest known Dumfriesshire arrival to the Island was James Mullins, who, came from Annan in 1798. He died at Tryon aged 94, having raised 17 children.[14] In addition to people like James Mullins who emigrated directly from Scotland, there may well have been some

FOR RICHIBUCTO, MIRAMICHI, CHA-
LUER BAY, and ST. JOHN'S ISLAND,
NOVA SCOTIA, NORTH AMERICA,

THE Brig NANCY, of Dum-
fries, only 4 years old, burden about 400 tons, Joseph Kirk,
master, will Sail from Glencaple
Quay, about the 1st of April curt.
The Vessel having undergone a
thorough alteration, will be found
a safe and comfortable conveyance for passengers; the Births
will he fitted up in the most comfortable manner, and there
will be provided abundance of water and fuel for the voyage;
and the kind attentions of Capt. Kirk to the comfort of his
passengers are so well known as to render further comment
unnecessary. As a number are already engaged, immediate
application will be necessary.

P. S.—For Freight or Passage, apply to the Captain on
Board, or Mr John Carruthers, Blue Bell Inn, Friars' Ven-
nal, Dumfries.

Notice of the imminent departure of the *Nancy* from
Dumfries to St. John's Island (Prince Edward Island)
and other Maritime ports. *From* Dumfries and Galloway Courier, *12 March 1822.*

Dumfriesshire Loyalists who were resettled on the Island in the late
eighteenth century. The very fact that New Annan, named from Annan
in Dumfriesshire, is in lot 19 strongly hints at a sizeable Dumfriesshire
population in a township with Loyalist associations.[15] We would expect
any Dumfriesshire Loyalists in this area to have been relocated from
New York since this was the colony which attracted so many trades-
men and weavers from the southwest Borders during the mid-1770s.[16]

The people who sailed to the Island from Dumfriesshire and
Kirkcudbrightshire in 1774–1775 left no traces behind. It was primarily the parishes to the south, with good access to the port of Dumfries, which lost most people to these expeditions. Kirkcudbrightshire
emigrants tended to come from one of four parishes (Colvend, South-
wick, Kirkbean and New Abbey) while the Dumfriesshire emigrants
were far more widely scattered across many parishes (especially
Annan, Hoddam, Caerlaverock and St. Mungo).[17] Tombstone and
newspaper sources tell us that Dumfriesshire rather than Kirkcudbrightshire maintained lasting links with the Island. Amazingly, most

of the later Dumfriesshire arrivals originated from precisely those areas which had provided the 1774–1775 influx. Again we have another tantalizing clue pointing to an eighteenth century beginning for Dumfriesshire's associations with the Island, but no positive proof.

The desire to emigrate and the availability of cheap and regular overseas transport were not the only factors which led to the pronounced influx from Dumfriesshire to the eastern Maritimes just after the end of the Napoleonic Wars. There were also the opportunities to be had from being in a prime timber producing region. The Island's trade, although substantial, was minuscule when compared with New Brunswick's production levels. Eastern Nova Scotia and Prince Edward Island were among the first areas to be cleared for their timber but their relative importance declined by the 1820s, as New Brunswick came to dominate the field. It was along the Miramichi Bay and River, together with its tributaries, where Scots first became concentrated in large numbers.[18] The many Scottish-born farmers, merchants, shipwrights and storekeepers who appear in the 1851 *Census Returns* for the Miramichi area reflect the early dominance of Scots both as settlers and exploiters of the forest.[19] But we need to go a short distance south, along New Brunswick's eastern coastline into Kent County, to find many of our Dumfriesshire settlers, who began arriving in 1816. It was to Richibucto where many Dumfriesshire Scots were first drawn. From 1818, as its timber production began its rapid climb, Richibucto became the preferred choice of many Scottish, as well as Irish settlers.[20] A Presbyterian minister who visited the area in 1826 tells us that Richibucto had a thriving Church of Scotland congregation and was about to acquire its own church.[21] Some settled at Galloway, near Richibucto and many others further inland, in Weldford parish.[22] The name Galloway has strong associations with southwest Scotland. But the really solid evidence of a strong Dumfriesshire presence comes from the *New Brunswick Census.* This shows that, in 1861, around 30 to 40 percent of householders in these two areas claimed Scottish ancestry and that most emigrant Scots in Weldford parish (where county origins were recorded) originated from Dumfriesshire.[23]

Table 5: Emigrant Ship Crossings to British America
From Dumfries, 1816–1822*

*Sources: SRO E504/9/9, *Scots Magazine, Island Magazine, Dumfries and Galloway Courier and Herald, New Brunswick Royal Gazette, Quebec Mercury.*

Yr.	Mo.	Vessel	Master	No. of Psgrs	Arrival Port
1816	03	*Jessie* of Dumfries [The *Jessie* returned from St Andrews in July with a cargo of pine.]	Thomson, George	20	St Andrews N.B.
1816	06	*Lovely Mary* of Dumfries [The *Lovely Mary* was a small schooner (90 tons) of doubtful quality.]	Hudson, John	29	Pictou
1816	07	*Jessie* of Dumfries [Ship's second crossing to St Andrews in 1816.]	Williams, James	8	St Andrews
1816	07	*North Star* of Dumfries [The *North Star* was a very small schooner (83 tons). It was taken in wartime and almost rebuilt in 1811.]	Muir, James	12	Richibucto N.B.
1817	04	*Jessie* of Dumfries [Sailed again for St John N.B. in July]	Williams, James	67	St John N.B.
1817	04	*North Star* of Dumfries [Newspaper advertisement indicates 40 shilling deposit for fares; made 2 trips to Richibucto in 1817.]	Muir, James	33	Richibucto
1817	04	*Augusta* of Dumfries	Davidson, Wm.	115	Pictou, Miramichi, N.B.
1817	04	*Elizabeth* of Dumfries	Thomson, George	125	St John
1817	07	*General Goldie* of Dumfries [18 settlers left at Quebec. The *General Goldie* was a small sloop (61 tons) but in "A1" condition.]	Smith, Willam	18	Pictou, Quebec. Miramichi

1818	04	*Augusta* of Dumfries [66 chests wearing apparel; *Dumfries Weekly Journal* gave 56 passengers for Miramichi while the Customs Records show 120 passengers. The agent was John Thomson.]	Whitehead, Robert	120	Pictou, Miramichi
1818	04	*Elizabeth* of Dumfries [*Royal Gazette & Dumfries Journal* gave 149 passengers while the Customs Records show 110 passengers. The agent was John Thomson.]	Thomson, George	110	St John
1818	05	*Lovely Mary* of Dumfries	Hudson, John	53	Pictou
1818	05	*Nile* of Dumfries [The *Dumfries Journal* stated "those proceeding to Quebec will make immediate application as the number will very soon be made up from the great encouragement given to settlers in Upper Canada by the government."]	Carswell, Robert	39	Richibucto, Quebec
1818	05	*Thomson's Packet* of Dumfries [Goods for Philadelphia and 186 passengers for St John.]	Thomson, William	186	St John
1818	06	*Charlotte* of Dumfries	Gibson, James	27	St John
1818	06	*General Goldie* of Dumfries	Smith, William	30	Quebec
1818	06	*Nancy* of Dumfries	Kirk, Joseph	149	St John
1818	06	*Success* of Whitehaven		37	Miramichi
1818	08	*Jessie* of Dumfries [40 chests wearing apparel; according to the *Dumfries Journal*, the vessel left with 72 passengers but Customs Records show only 15.]	Williams, James	72	St John

1818	09	*Augusta* of Dumfries [Second crossing to New Brunswick in 1818.]		17	St John
1819	04	*Augusta* of Dumfries [See *Thomson's Packet*]		286	St John
1819	04	*Jessie* of Dumfries [See *Thomson's Packet*]	Williams, James		PEI, Miramichi
1819	04	*Thomson's Packet* of Dumfries [The *Thomson's Packet, Jessie* and *Augusta* together took 517 passengers; the *Dumfries and Galloway Courier* claimed that a total of £18, 000 had been taken out by them; agent was John Thomson; passengers described as labourers & small farmers; the group included people from the North of England.]		150	St John
1820	04	*Diana* of Dumfries [Forty-three passengers arrived at Charlottetown.]	Martin, John	43	PEI, Chaleur Bay
1820	04	*Jessie* of Dumfries [The *Dumfries Weekly Journal* noted that the vessel left with 179 passengers.]	Williams, James	179	PEI, Miramichi Richibucto
1820	04	*Thomson's Packet* Dumfries	Lookup, T.	111	St John, St Andrews
1820	04	*Britannia* of Dumfries [The *Dumfries Weekly Journal* stated that the *Britannia* left with 90 passengers.]	McDowall	90	PEI, Miramichi
1820	05	*Elizabeth* of Dumfries	Carruthers, John	76	St John
1820	06	*Martha*	Denwood, Joseph	43	Quebec
1820	07	*Argus* [*The Quebec Mercury* recorded that 73 passengers arrived at Quebec.]	Wilkinson, Wm.	88	Quebec

1821	04	*Elizabeth* of Dumfries [The *Royal Gazette* stated that 176 passengers arrived at St John.]	Thomson, G.	165	St John
1821	04	*Diana* of Dumfries [53 passengers left at Charlottetown.]	Martin, John	53	PEI, Chaleur Bay
1821	04	*Thomson's Packet* of Dumfries [Eighty passengers are known to have left at Pictou.]		80	PEI, Miramichi, Pictou, Richibucto
1821	05	*Nancy* of Dumfries [Goods and 15 passengers were noted by the *Dumfries and Galloway Courier.*]	Kirk, Joseph	15	PEI, Miramichi,
1822	04	*Diana* of Dumfries [Sixteen passengers disembarked at Charlottetown.]	Martin, John	16	PEI, Chaleur Bay
1822	05	*Elizabeth* of Dumfries	Whitehead	100	St John
1822	05	*Thomson's Packet* of Dumfries [40 emigrants went on to Quebec.]	Lookup, T.	133	Pictou & Quebec
1822	08	*Swallow* [The *Dumfries Courier* claimed most emigrants came from Cumbria and reported unfavourably on their departure; some were weavers.]	Davidson, Wm.	65	St John

The Census also tells us that the Scottish presence in these areas had been greatly enhanced by substantial migration from Prince Edward Island. The Northumberland Strait is about all that separates Richibucto from the principal concentrations of Dumfriesshire settlers on the Island (lots 17, 19, 25, 26, 28 and 29). Thus it was that by travelling a relatively short distance across the Strait these settlers could take advantage of the new opportunities to be had in timber production along New Brunswick's eastern coastline and river tributaries.[24]

Judging from the small number of recorded emigrant ship crossings from Dumfries to Richibucto (two in 1816, and one in 1818), we can infer that Richibucto acquired much of its Dumfriesshire population from Prince Edward Island rather than Scotland (Table 5). Whatever attractions the Island may have had initially, the prospect of the better economic opportunities to be in the Richibucto area clearly outweighed all other factors.

The regular trade links forged between Dumfries and the Maritimes thus had the effect of pulling Dumfriesshire emigrants to this region but the phenomenon was relatively short-lived. By 1830, with the coming of larger ships and more centralised transport, emigrant departures from the port of Dumfries diminished. The Cumbrian ports of Maryport, Workington and Whitehaven took over as the main overseas passenger departures ports for the southwest of Scotland and by this time, Upper Canada had become the preferred destination of most emigrants.

During the nine or so years, when the emigrant trade from the port of Dumfries was brisk, the dominant shipper was John Thomson. He launched himself in 1812 when he established his brothers in branch offices in New Brunswick and Liverpool.[25] His ships regularly took emigrants from Dumfries to Prince Edward Island, as well as to the Miramichi, Richibucto and Chaleur Bay regions of New Brunswick, and returned with timber.[26] In the peak emigration period, Thomson ran two to three passenger-carrying ships each year, with the *Jessie* and *Thompson's Packet* being regular stalwarts (Table 5). They were less than five years old when they first took passengers to the Island and had first-class, (or "A1") designations.[27] This was the general pattern for most emigrant ships which sailed to the Island from Dumfries (Appendix II). New and high quality ships are highly significant. Shippers like Thomson had to beat the competition from bigger ports such as the Clyde, and to do this they had to offer their best ships.

New Annan (lot 19) is a lasting reminder of the Island's Dumfriesshire roots as is Bonshaw, in the Tryon area just to the southeast of Crapaud (lot 29). Both names appear to have originated with prominent Dumfriesshire businessmen, whose contact with the Island was

For Prince Edward's Island and Pictou.

THE BRIG DIANA, John
Martin, Master, burden
per Register 226 Tons, will sail
from Carsethorn, on Saturday the
12th August, This Vessel having
very superior accommodation, will
be found a comfortable conveyance for Passengers.
    Apply to.   JOHN WALKER & SON.
N. B.—Persons wishing to purchase Land in Prince Edward's Island, may learn particulars by application as above.

PINE TIMBER.

JUST arrived, and now discharging at Carse-
thorn, a CARGO of excellent YELLOW
PINE TIMBER, LATHWOOD, &c. ex the
Diana, John Martin, from Prince Edward's Island.
    Apply to   JOHN WALKER & SON.
Dumfries, 25th July, 1820.

Notice of the arrival at Dumfries, of the *Diana* with a
timber cargo from Prince Edward Island and notifica-
tion of the return journey back to Pictou and the
Island. People wishing to travel to, or buy land in
Prince Edward Island should contact the local agent,
John Walker & Son. *Fom the* Dumfries Weekly
Journal, *1 August 1820.*

relatively late. New Annan is thought to have been named by Squire
Jamieson, who built mills in the area sometime in the 1830s. Bonshaw's
founder, Mr. W.W. Irving, from Bonshaw Tower in Dumfries, also came
on the scene about this time. Acquiring a substantial holding which he
dubbed the Bonshaw estate, Irving sought Dumfriesshire settlers for
his land by advertising in local newspapers.[28] The presence of these
men would have stimulated some emigration from Dumfriesshire to the
Island and, although small in absolute terms, would have been a strong
factor in the county's continuing endorsement of the Island even as late
as the 1840s.

If it had not been for its Dumfriesshire settlers, the Island's Scottish
intake would have consisted almost solely of emigrants from Argyll

and the northwest Highlands and Islands. The southwest Borders, and especially Dumfriesshire, were quite unique in being the only areas of Lowland Scotland to lose substantial numbers to Prince Edward Island. This had happened primarily because Dumfries' early trading links with British America were primarily centred around the eastern Maritimes. But from the 1830s the picture changed dramatically. With the coming of railways, better roadways and new canal systems on both sides of the Atlantic, together with the introduction of the steamship, transport ceased to restrict emigrant destination choices to any great extent. As a wider world opened up to people in the southwest Borders, the Island could no longer compete with Upper Canada's better climate and economic opportunities and the Dumfriesshire influx became a trickle.

At the time when Dumfriesshire's links with the Island were receding, the Island once again experienced a large influx from Skye. The many who arrived in 1829–1830 were followed by even larger numbers in the following decade. These groups marked the end of an era. Scots would continue to arrive singly or in small groups, but the days when entire boatloads from a Scottish Island would come to the Island *en masse* were soon to end.

VI

LATER ARRIVALS FROM SKYE

"Eighty-four emigrants, including women and children, from the
Isle of Skye arrived here [Prince Edward Island] on Sunday.
They left their native place about six weeks ago in a ship for
Cape Breton along with a number of settlers for that Island.
They seem all to be in high health and judging
from appearance in easy circumstances.
With prudent foresight characteristic of their race they came
provided with 12 months provisions and an ample stock
of warm clothing. They have all relatives already settled
in the Island chiefly about Belfast, and with the exception
of one family it is, we understand, their intention
to locate in that thriving settlement."[1]

THE *Prince Edward Island Gazette's* announcement of the arrival,
in 1829, of eighty-four families from Skye, who had sailed on the *Mary
Kennedy,* had an optimistic ring.[2] This was a well-turned out group of
emigrants, who had come with ample provisions. Far from being a
potential drain on local resources, the unspoken message was that
these people would be an asset to the Island. The *Vestal* followed soon
after, in August of that same year, with still more settlers from Skye.
These were probably the ships which attracted such favourable coverage from the *Inverness Journal.* According to its report, these emi-

grants were in the hands of "two respectable agents—Islesmen themselves" who were from Skye. The newspaper hinted that a deal sympathetic to the interests of the emigrants had been struck, reporting that the necessary ships had been chartered "partly as a trading speculation and partly an act of philanthropy...not uncommon among better orders in the Highlands."[3] Most were heading for Orwell Bay, to lay claim to a large amount of vacant land in lot 50, which they had been able to acquire. They immediately dubbed their settlement Uigg.[4] It was an appropriate choice since a large proportion of them originated from Uig in the north east of Skye.

A reporter on the other side of the Atlantic, might have described things differently. With the collapse of the kelp industry from the mid-1820s, the Highland economy, always fragile even at the best of times, was on its knees. Against this background, we might have expected a Scottish reporter to tell us that a pitiful and confused group of down-and-outs from Skye were on their way to the Island. But instead we read that eighty-four Skye families arrived in a good state and even gave the impression of being "in easy circumstances." However good an impression they may have made, the fact remained that with the demise of kelp, poverty and lack of opportunity at home would have triggered this large exodus from Skye.

Ironically, kelp had previously been the Highlands and Island's greatest asset.[5] Kelp production had been rising steadily in Skye, Mull, the Outer Hebrides and in parts of Argyll from the 1770s. It had been a highly profitable source of income for Scottish landowners and an essential provider of labour for their tenantry. It had helped to arrest the dislocating effect of the advancing sheep farms and encouraged population growth in the region. But unfortunately the population increase it fostered became unsustainable, with catastrophic consequences. Matters came to a head in the 1820s with the general industrial depression and the demise of kelp production. Countless people were in an extreme state of destitution. Alternative employment opportunities were almost non-existent and most people faced the prospect of relocation. It is hardly surprising then that nearly every

Uig Bay, Skye. The squat round tower in the foreground is a folly c. 1840. Large numbers left Uigg in 1829 to found Uigg in Prince Edward Island. *Photograph taken in 1931, courtesy of St. Andrews University Library.*

Scot who came to Prince Edward Island in the late 1820s and early 1830s originated from one of the kelp producing areas in the Western Isles. In 1829 alone, nearly 200 emigrants arrived from the Outer Hebrides and at least 600 came from Skye. Between 1829 and 1831 at least eight ships arrived with large numbers of emigrants. Most had sailed directly from Tobermory, Skye or Stornoway (Appendix II).[6]

The build-up to this large surge in emigration had begun in Skye from the mid-1820s. Some families faced actual evictions.[7] For many, the least bad option was a new life abroad. As conditions deteriorated many Highlanders chose to sell up and go:

> "Their whole property consists of black cattle and small horses all of which are made over to the emigration agents at his own risk and which he sends to the southern markets at his own risk...the roof of their huts, their boats, in short everything they have must be converted into money by him before the necessary sum for defraying the freight can be realised."[8]

The issue for these desperately poor people therefore, was not whether they should emigrate, but rather whether they could raise sufficient capital to pay for their relocation. Proprietors at this time rarely subsidised emigration although most encouraged it. Gone were the days when landlords fought hard to retain their tenants in the face of mounting enthusiasm for a new life abroad. Some landlords even came to view emigration as a low cost means of dispensing with unwanted tenantry. But few landlords in the 1820s and 1830s offered to help their tenants with their travel costs so most were left to their own devices. In desperation, many sought help from the government. Typical of the deluge of requests sent to the Colonial Office was this petition from families in Bracadale, Skye. The threat of eviction hung over them:

> "They and their fathers occupied small farms in the above parish [Bracadale, Skye], but their landlord having consolidated these farms let them to two persons for sheep-walks, and the petitioners are to quit their houses at Whitsunday 1826, but they have no place to remove to in the Isle of Skye which is already too populous. That deprived of their farms they are unable to provide for themselves and families or to pay their passage to Canada."[9]

The government received thousands of petitions like this and all were turned down. In the end, these Bracadale families would have had to raise funds to finance their relocation themselves. To do so meant that they had to have time to plan and organise.

Lord MacDonald's Skye tenants, who arrived on the Island in 1829, would have been in much the same quandary as the Bracadale families. The probability is that they were encouraged to emigrate by their landlord, although there is no evidence of any force being used. Their prospects may have been bleak, but they had not been pushed into making quick decisions. They had time to raise funds for their passages and judging from the *Gazette*'s glowing report, their expedition had been carefully planned. There was no air of panic. Quite the opposite. This was a well-organized group, who had managed to acquire a prime site on the Island. Their chosen site lay adjacent to Belfast, which had its roots in the Selkirk-funded expedition of 1803. To acquire large acreages in one consolidated area in a single township, and in a good location, would have been quite a feat in itself, given the complexities and infuriating idiosyncrasies of the Island's near feudal land system. But, to have landed such a prized settlement site, next to the principal Skye footholds at Belfast, these emigrants needed more than exceptionally good contacts. They also needed time to steer themselves through the Island's bureaucratic procedures and time to plan, negotiate for land and raise funds.

The 1829 contingent from Skye prospered and attracted further re-enforcements from Skye in later years. Like the Belfast settlers who had preceded them by some thirty years, these Uigg settlers were groups of extended families who, even before they set foot on the Island, functioned as a cohesive self-supporting community. Included in this influx from Skye was the Rev. Samuel MacLeod, who stood out as result of his conversion from Presbyterianism to the Baptist faith.[10] He established a highly successful Baptist ministry on the Island and by using a version of the Gaelic Psalms approved by the Church of Scotland, he won wide acceptance within Highland communities, in spite of their affiliations with Presbyterianism.[11] A charismatic personality thus mattered more than strict observances of faith within close-knit pioneer communities. Old world identities also mattered. Tombstone inscriptions at Uigg echo treasured links with a former life in Skye:

"MacLeod, Here rest from their labours after enduring and overcoming the hardships of early settlement in this colony, Roderick MacLeod, born in the Isle of Skye, Scotland came to P.E. Island in 1829 and died 29 June, 1882 aged 85. Also Catherine, his dearly beloved wife who died 2 December, 1882, aged 75."

"Norman MacLeod, 1762–1837. Margaret MacPhee, his second wife, 1778–1855. Both born in Isle of Skye, Scotland. Stone erected on the occasion of the Uigg centenary, 1929...."

"Donald Munroe, died May 24, 1873, aged 80. Also his wife, Mary, died May 8, 1891, aged 92. Natives of Uigg, Isle of Skye, Scotland."[12]

Portree in Skye c. 1888. A great many of the Skye settlers who came to the Island originated from Portree and areas directly to the north (Snizort and Kilmuir). *Copyright George Washington Wilson Collection, Aberdeen University, E3673.*

Uigg attracted considerable numbers throughout the 1830s and 1840s from the northeast of Skye. Most were tenants from the MacDonald estate who originated mainly from Kilmuir, Snizort and Portree. Emigration numbers peaked in 1839–1840 as economic conditions worsened. The country had experienced a severe depression in the early 1830s, while a succession of bad harvests led to a severe famine in the Highlands in 1837 and 1838. By 1841, when Scotland's economic and social problems had become particularly acute, the government was again being forced to look at the feasibility of using public money to facilitate emigration. Once more it resisted these pressures. But a new development in the working of the Scottish Poor Law was to have enormous repercussions in stimulating further emigration from the Highlands. The 1845 Poor Law Amendment Act, which for the first time made proprietors legally responsible for any destitute people on their land, gave landlords a strong incentive to assist their tenants to emigrate. This they did on a large scale from the early 1840s.[13]

Six ships took well over 2,000 people from the Western Isles to Prince Edward Island in the three years from 1839 to 1841. Unlike the people who came in the late 1820s and 1830s, these emigrants got help with their transport costs. Most were tenants of Lord MacDonald. Around two thirds originated from Skye and the remainder from North Uist. The North Uist emigrants were taken in 1839-1840 from Stornoway on two ships, the *Pekin* of Liverpool and the *Heroine* of Aberdeen. Together they carried around 600 passengers. The remaining four ships, the *Nith, Rother, Ocean* of Liverpool and *Washington* of Liverpool sailed in 1840–1841 and together carried around 1,700 passengers (Appendix II). A carefully documented account of the funds given to each person reveals that 1,621 individuals from Skye and 841 from North Uist received financial help to emigrate. The total amount granted was £2,250 or roughly £1 per person, with Lord MacDonald's contribution being matched by funds received from the Edinburgh and Glasgow Highland Relief Fund Committees.[14] However, given that adult steerage fares at the time were around £4, these emigrants were only given help towards their fares and thus still had to raise considerable sums themselves.[15]

As was the case a decade earlier, there is a wide gulf between the perceived state of mind of these people when they left, and the impression they made on arrival on the Island. Most Scottish documentary sources are based on government enquiries and estate papers which deal almost solely with problems of destitution and the need for subsidies to assist people to emigrate. In this three year period we had a large exodus of extremely poor people from a single estate who got assisted passages from their landlord. It would be tempting to conclude that this is *prima facie* evidence of a wholesale clearance of surplus tenantry, packed off by a heartless landlord to North America, not for their benefit, but because he wanted rid of them. This is certainly the view which is commonly held by many commentators.[16] But evidence from the other side of the Atlantic tell us to be wary of jumping too quickly to such conclusions.

When the *Rother* arrived in 1840 with "229 passengers, all natives of the Isle of Skye" the *Prince Edward Island Gazette* observed that:

"They seemed all in robust health and we have no doubt they will prove themselves to be a hardy industrious class of settlers."[17]

When just a few days later the *Nith* arrived with 315 passengers from Skye, this same newspaper reported that:

"We understand the chief part of them have some property and are likely to be good settlers."[18]

We are left with an impression of positively-motivated people, not of poor bedraggled beggars expecting some dreadful fate in Prince Edward Island.

But even more compelling evidence comes from the emigrants themselves. Tombstones and death notices tell us where they decided to take up land and settle. Many went to Belfast (lot 57), Murray Harbour (lot 64) in the south eastern extremity of the Belfast area and to Breadalbane (lot 67), located much further away to the west.[19] Dundas (lot 55) also attracted Skye emigrants—particularly from Kilmuir, even though it was a strongly Roman Catholic area, having been originally settled by South Uist emigrants from as early as 1790.[20] All of these locations had one thing in common. They were all in or close to well-established Scottish communities.

The overwhelming conclusion we are driven to is that these people planned their relocation on the Island in a very measured and determined way. This behaviour pattern is inconsistent with the presumption that they were forced out against their will. People in such circumstances would not have had the stomach for deliberate and careful planning, nor made such a positive impression upon their arrival on the Island. They did not see emigration as some random leap into the unknown at someone else's behest. They carefully planned their own departures and through their Island contacts, located large holdings of vacant land in

areas close to fellow Scots. It was a group response by which entire communities relocated themselves to places on the Island which already nur-
tured their traditions and culture.[21] The offer of an assisted passage was
something to be snapped up rather than feared, particularly if it offered
an escape from extreme poverty and a hopeless future.

Skye emigrants had a long-enduring attachment to the Maritimes
which put them in a different category from most others. With the
enormous strides being made in better transport from the 1830s,
Upper Canada beckoned most Scots, since its land, climate and
employment opportunities had far more to offer. But during the 1830s
and 1840s large numbers from Skye chose the Island. When John
Bowie, who had managed the business affairs of extensive Highland
estates for some 12 years, was called to give evidence before the 1841
Emigration Select Committee, he gave this account of the special
appeal which Prince Edward Island and Cape Breton held for Skye
settlers:

"Since 1837, I have with reference to estates [on Skye], been the
means of removing a population of 1,850; 600 of those were con-
veyed to Australia at the Government's expense, the remaining
1,250 have gone to our North American possessions, principally to
Prince Edward's Island and Cape Breton. The parties preferred
those districts in consequence of many of their countrymen having
previously settled there; and in consequence of the representations
sent home to them, last year there were 700 or 800 went from Skye;
and the parties had not been long in their new country before they
wrote home such favourable accounts to their friends, that parties
are now anxious and many are now actually arranging to go out as
soon as they can procure the means."[22]

As far as it went this was an accurate explanation, but it is not complete. Skye's amazing links with Prince Edward Island were quite
unique. Skye was one of the earliest parts of the Western Isles to catch
the "epidemical fury of emigration" noted so cogently by Johnson and

Boswell as they travelled through Skye in 1773.[23] At the time, most Skye emigration was directed towards North Carolina. The 1803 contingents, led by Lord Selkirk, ensured that the so-called "fury of emigration" became targeted at Prince Edward Island instead of North Carolina. But Lord Selkirk's intervention did more than just establish the initial links between Skye and the Island. His choice of Angus MacAuley, a former factor on Lord MacDonald's Skye estates, to recruit emigrants ensured that the take-up would be concentrated in this one part of Skye. Hence the preponderance of settlers from Kilmuir, Snizort and Portree, in the northeast of Skye. It was they, who in effect, created "new world" versions of their homeland which attracted the considerable numbers over four decades.

Although emigration offered the means to preserve culture and lifestyle, it was a painful choice. Selkirk backed these settlers from the Western Isles because he knew they could take the privations of pioneer life and they, in the end, succeeded. The first generation had a diet of heartache and grinding work but for the generations who followed, the rewards were plentiful. It is fitting that Selkirk's memorial should lie close to the many tombstones of the early pioneering families at Belfast. It was a remarkable team effort. However, the tinge of melancholy in the eulogy to Lord Selkirk reminds us that success came at a price:

"In memory of Thomas Douglas Selkirk the 5th Earl of Selkirk, philanthropist and colonizer, who believing that the hardships of the Scottish Highland peasantry could be alleviated only by emigration came to Canada in 1803 and established a large settlement in this area."

VII

LEAKY TUBS OR FIRST CLASS SHIPS?

"Being all ready on 18th April [1820], on board the brig *Diana* of
Dumfries, we sailed next morning at four o'clock, from the foot of
the river Nith. All the passengers, forty-five in number, later became
more or less seasick. On the 28th day we saw American land,
supposedly the south side of Cape Breton, but the fog was so thick we
could only discern the shore, and had to stand out to sea and steer
backwards and forwards on the banks of Newfoundland for eight days.
When it cleared, passing Cape North, we entered the Gulf
of St. Lawrence. On Friday morning we made Prince Edward Island
about nine o'clock, rising like a dark cloud from the bosom of the ocean.
Approaching the shore we discovered little clearances here and there,
next [to] the houses. About three o'clock we were so near as to require
a pilot. Three young men came in a canoe cut from a solid tree.
Their dress consisted of jacket and trousers, all of Island manufacture,
like Scotch blanketing, home-dyed blue. They wore moccasins and,
upon the whole, had rather a rough appearance, but discovered great
agility, polished manners and spoke English as fine as Londoners.
This was Three Rivers."[1]

NONE OF US today will ever experience, first hand, what Walter
Johnstone saw as Three Rivers came into view in the Spring of 1820.
His excitement at reaching the end is understandable and well-
described, although somewhat racy in style. Considering that, in addi-

tion to enduring sea-sickness, he and his 42 fellow passengers had to sit tight while the *Diana* sailed backwards and forwards off the Newfoundland coast for eight days to wait for fog to lift, he was in remarkably good spirits. Most of the passengers would have anticipated their safe arrival. The *Diana* was a top-grade, one-year-old ship. We do not know whether her passengers felt that she had lived up to her advance billing as "a most desirable conveyance," but she did take further emigrant cargoes over the next two years to the Island under the direction of the same Captain, John Martin.[2]

The *Diana* was one of many new vessels built during the great ship building boom created by the explosive growth in the North American timber trade. From 1816 even small ports like Dumfries had developed their own trade links and acquired purpose-built ships to transport timber supplies from the Maritime forests. Ships like the *Diana* of Dumfries made regular crossings across the Atlantic from their home port to collect timber, and when they were available, took emigrants on their outward journeys. Having taken Walter Johnstone and others to the Island in the Spring of 1820, the *Diana* returned to Dumfries in late July with a "cargo of excellent yellow pine timber, lathwood etc., from Prince Edward Island." A few days later, the *Diana's* agent was touting for business in the *Dumfries Weekly Journal*. She would be sailing back to Prince Edward Island on Saturday, 12th August, having "very superior accommodation" for passengers and "persons wishing to purchase land in Prince Edward Island" could get details from the shipping agent.[3] This is graphic evidence of the two-way traffic in timber and people being fostered by the North American timber trade. However, not all emigrants had ready access to major sea ports; yet they too benefited from the growing number of Atlantic crossings from Britain.

The major influx to Prince Edward Island was from the Highlands and Islands—an area with virtually no foreign timber trade connections. While there was no question of ships making round trips from Tobermory or Stornoway, with passengers one way and timber the other, a well-developed passenger service had sprung into action, which made use of spare capacity on westward-bound shipping. The *Louisa* of Aberdeen and *Heroine* of Aberdeen, sailing in 1829 and 1840 respectively, were typical of the ships which occasionally called at ports in the Western Isles to collect passengers on their way across the Atlantic (Appendix II).[4] Because large numbers were involved in the exodus from Skye, it was relatively easy to attract shippers with spare capacity. In diverting their ships to the Western Isles, the owners of the Aberdeen-registered *Loiusa* and *Heroine* obtained far more passengers in a single crossing than they would normally hope to get from the Aberdeen catchment area in several years.[5] The sizeable numbers also attracted shippers from English ports like Hull and Liverpool. The *Clarendon* of Hull which sailed from Oban in 1808 with 208 passengers from Perthshire and Argyll, and the *Washington* of Liverpool, sailing in 1841 with 551 passengers from Skye, beat the Scottish competition in the bidding for transatlantic passengers. They were fleeting and opportunistic participants in the Scottish emigrant trade, probably capitalising on their substantial size and competitive fares.[6]

Only a small proportion of the ships which were used in the Atlantic timber trade ever carried passengers. Through the *Lloyd's Shipping Register* we can actually assess the quality of the individual ships which were used to take emigrants from Scotland to Prince Edward Island. Dating back to the late eighteenth century, it offers a unique and highly reliable indicator of the quality of the individual ships in use year by year.[7] We find that emigrant shipping was not, as is generally believed, concentrated on the poorest ships. Quite the reverse. The data for Prince Edward Island arrivals, although incomplete, shows that emigrants generally sailed on good quality ships. With the possible exception of one ship, the *Lovelly Nelly,* which sailed in 1774 and 1775 with passengers from the southwest Borders, the standard of shipping was generally good and in many cases the best available.[8]

As major insurers, Lloyd's needed reliable shipping intelligence, which it procured through the use of paid agents in the main ports in Britain and abroad. Whether they insured their ships with Lloyd's or not, shipowners wishing to attract cargoes offered their ships for

Oban Harbour viewed from the southwest. In 1806–1808, four ships took emigrants to the Island from Oban. *Photograph, registered 1880, courtesy of St. Andrews
University Library.*

inspection in order to signal their availability in the shipping market
place. Their ships thus became liable for a survey and the assignment
of a Lloyd's shipping code which categorised them according to the
quality of their construction and materials used, as well as their condition and age.[9] The codes had high commercial significance to both
insurers and shipowners. An honest and open inspection was vital to
the insurer's risk assessment, and the shipowner's ability to attract
profitable trade hinged on the classification given to his ships.
Shipowners actually criticised the system for being too stringent, particularly in the way a ship's age and place of construction could affect
its classification.[10] The maritime community consisted of hard-nosed
commercially minded people who dealt in fact, not half-truths or misty
anecdotal reflections. Ship classification codes were their legacy and
these tell us that the ships which carried emigrants tended to be at the
better end of the available shipping market.[11]

Ship identification is not an exact science owing to gaps and inconsistencies in shipping data sources.[12] In all, classification codes have been located for 43 of the 75 ships covered in this study representing a 57 per cent sample (Appendix II).[13] Thus we have a substantial proportion, but not a complete picture upon which to base conclusions on the overall quality of emigrant ships. Twenty five of the 43 ships with known codes, had an "A" ranking (first class construction and condition and recently built), while the remainder were ranked just below the top classification.[14] They had no defects, but their age put them beyond the reach of an A1 designation. No examples were found of ships which failed to get a classification and only one, the *Lovelly Nelly*, was assigned a code indicating its unsuitability or unsafeness. Far from being fobbed off with the worst shipping, emigrants were offered a consistently good quality of shipping. They were highly profitable to ship owners and the over-capacity of westward-bound shipping meant that shippers had to compete for their business.

Shipowners went to considerable lengths to locate passengers and depended on regional newspapers to convey details of crossings and ships. This advertisement, published in the *Dumfries and Galloway Courier* is a typical example:

"For Richibucto, Mirimachi, Chaleur Bay, and St. John['s] Island, Nova Scotia, North America; The brig *Nancy* of Dumfries, only 4 years old, burden about 400 tons, Joseph Kirk, master, will sail from Glencaple Quay about the 1st April. The vessel having undergone a thorough alteration will be found a safe and comfortable conveyance for passengers; the berths will be fitted up in the most comfortable manner, and there will be provided an abundance of water and fuel for the voyage; and the kind attentions of Captain Kirk to the comfort of his passengers are so well known to render further comment unnecessary."[15]

It was this reliance of the emigrant trade on the timber vessel that helped to justify the continuation of the preferential tariff arrangements which so favoured North American timber.[16] The practice of linking emigrant and timber transport spawned a network of emigration agencies which undertook to locate passengers and to manage their transport arrangements on behalf of individual shipowners.

Agents ran offices in large urban conurbations such as Glasgow, Leith and Aberdeen, where the pulling power of the port was sufficient to draw an ample and regular supply of passengers for westward bound timber ships. Eventually shippers, operating from large ports in the northwest of England, extended their reach into the west Border counties of Dumfriesshire and Roxburgh by employing emigration agents in Annan, Langholm, Moffat and Hawick to locate passengers for transatlantic crossings. However, emigrant shipping in the Highlands worked quite differently, in the sense that shippers came to the emigrant. Here emigrant demand was sufficiently high to entice shippers, with empty ships to fill on their outward journeys, to divert their ships from their home ports to the Highlands, to collect emigrants *en route* to crossing the Atlantic.

Except for the Dumfries registered ships which did regular return journeys to the Island (particularly from 1816 to 1822), most emigrant ships which arrived at Prince Edward Island from Scotland made a once only appearance. Although they made fleeting appearances, the emigration agents who procured them did not. They served for many years in their part of Scotland as the trusted middlemen who got the ships when groups of people were ready to leave. The agents' skill was in co-ordinating emigrant demand with shipping supply. They had a vested interest in doing repeat business and they could only do so if they offered good ships.

Agents were much vilified at the time for exploiting emigrants.[17] However, the agent depended just as much as a ship's captain or anyone else who made his livelihood from the emigrant trade on a good "word of mouth" recommendation. The evidence shows that most ships crossed the Atlantic without incident and the people who ran the trade from the emigration agent down to the sea captain tended to be highly reputable. For at least twenty years, Archibald MacNiven was

Stornoway Harbour viewed from Gallows Hill. The *Northern Friends* sailed from Stornoway in 1805 to the Island with emigrants. *Photograph, registered 1878, courtesy of St. Andrews University Library.*

the principal emigration agent in the Inner Hebrides and the adjacent mainland areas along the west coast. In 1841, he claimed that for the previous twenty years he had arranged ships for 16,000 people in the Highlands and Islands who had emigrated to Upper Canada, Nova Scotia, Prince Edward Island and Cape Breton. That was a track record of someone who knew how to satisfy his customers.[18]

A good quality ship does not in itself guarantee a comfortable crossing. Overcrowding was often excessive, particularly during the great surges in emigration in the late eighteenth and early nineteenth centuries. In fact, it was widespread concerns over the suffering caused by overcrowded emigrant ships which mobilised the Highland Society of Edinburgh to campaign for changes in the legislation governing passenger travel by sea.[19] The 1803 Passenger Act, stipulating minimum space and food requirements was duly passed by the government.[20] One of its principal regulations was that a ship's passenger load should be calculated on the basis of one person (irrespective of age) for every two tons, thus greatly reducing the numbers of passengers which shipowners had been accustomed to taking on their ships. The immediate effect of the new legislation can be seen in ship arrivals to the Island. Before 1803 typical examples included the 79 ton *Edinburgh* of Campbeltown, which sailed with around 100 passengers, the 148 ton *Mally* of Greenock with 236 people and the 284 ton *Polly* with 400 passengers. This space allowance represented even less than one ton per passenger. But by 1806 the picture had changed totally. The new, two tons per passenger, formula was very much in evidence when the 296 ton *Rambler* of Leith arrived at Charlottetown with only 130 passengers and the 330 ton *Spencer* of Newcastle with just 114 passengers.

However, this era was short-lived. There was a temporary reduction in passenger numbers, but the Act came to be widely ignored since the absence of a regulatory agency meant that it was unenforceable. It had ostensibly been passed as a humanitarian measure, but its real effect had been to price transatlantic travel out of the reach of ordinary people. When emigration levels began their steep rise with the ending of the Napoleonic Wars, the government succumbed to pressure from shipowners and agents, to allow vessels to carry less food and more people by passing legislation in 1817 which weakened the requirements of the 1803 Act. These changes were hailed in some quarters as a great step forward for emigrants because they enabled ship owners to reduce their fares:

"We are anxious to state what we believe is not generally known, that the Bill which has recently had the Royal assent gives great facilities to persons who are desirous of proceeding as settlers to…. North America, in as much, as by reducing the tonnage to be allowed to each individual during the passage it enables the masters of vessels…to take passengers at a much lower rate than has been hitherto demanded."[21]

Large numbers of emigrants once again arrived on the Island and shippers clearly had few qualms about filling their ships to levels reminiscent of the pre-1803 days. The 141 ton *Morningfield* of Aberdeen, sailing in 1819, with her 264 emigrants from Tobermory was a particularly extreme example. Then there were small vessels like the *General*

Goldie of Dumfries (61 tons) and the *North Star* of Dumfries (83 tons), which had been drafted into service as overseas passenger carriers to meet the burgeoning demand between 1816 and 1822 from emigrants in the southwest Borders (Table 5). Although they were primarily intended for the coastal and fishing trade, their *Lloyd's Register* classifications reveal that both were built to withstand the rigours of long overseas journeys.[22] Subsequent legislation, enacted in 1823, to tighten up the regulations was again repealed in 1827 in response to continuing commercial pressures.

The large Skye contingents, which arrived on the Island from 1829 to 1833, were one small part of the great exodus taking place at the time from Scotland to British America. Little is known about the ships which arrived on the Island at this time. It was a period characterised by low fares and a rapidly growing interest in the opportunities to be had in Upper Canada. Most emigrants were heading for Quebec and, apart from the Skye settlers, the Island held little attraction for Scots. We know more about the ships which arrived during the next great surge of Skye arrivals to the Island in 1840–1841. Ships like the *Pekin* of Liverpool, the *Rother* and the *Heroine* of Aberdeen each carried large numbers, with a space allocation averaging about one ton per passenger—half the amount stipulated in the 1803 Act. Throughout this time emigrants had to cope with an unregulated service which theoretically left them at the mercy of unscrupulous shipowners and captains. However, their desire for repeat business was a powerful check against unsavoury practices and was certainly far more effective than any of the government's attempts to regulate overseas travel. In 1817, a year when demand was very high, some shippers complained of a customer price ceiling. Donald MacCrummer, an emigration agent based in Skye, told the Colonial Office that the "kilted heroes of Waterloo" could not afford his fares at £6 or £7, but if the tonnage restrictions were reduced from 2 tons per passenger to 1 ton per passenger, he could reduce his fares to what they can afford—£4 or £5.[23] Shippers were interested in high volume where they could find it, so their strategy was to set prices at a level which they thought most emigrants could afford. In the end, the government gave in to their demands. The result was that, until well into the 1830s, shipowners could adopt a low price, high volume policy which relied on getting people safely across the Atlantic but with few frills.[24] This suited most emigrants who put a much higher premium on having low fares than on their creature comforts.

Before 1810 most emigrant ship arrivals to the Island were from Scotland. By the 1820s most ships came from England and Ireland and hardly any were from Scotland. Throughout this period we have irrefutable evidence that ships of consistently high quality were used. Emigrants may have had melancholy crossings but few sailed in leaky or excessively overcrowded ships.[25] There were occasional shipwrecks and wretched crossings, particularly of ships from Ireland during the famine years between 1846 and 1851.[26] However, contrary to popular depiction, casualties at sea were infrequent occurrences. The picture of the emigrant as a compliant customer of a rapacious shipowner, travelling in a worn-out, disease-ridden tub, at the mercy of an uncaring captain, is not borne out by the evidence.

VIII

He Thinks Himself Already A Prince

"The passion and imagination of the Highland cottager are
so far aroused as to give him day-dreams of a lairdship and
an air-built castle of his own in Prince Edward's Island…
[he] thinks himself already a Prince."[1]

THESE GRANDIOSE NOTIONS seem ridiculous now but in 1810, in
the hard fought propaganda battles over emigration, this was just one
of many feeble attempts to stop the unstoppable. As this account from
Thomas Wilson of Charlottetown shows, emigrants were not following silly pipe dreams, but had very down-to-earth expectations of what
constituted a better life:

"I am happy you have heard from our sister Cathron and that they
are all well and doing well but there is great opportunity of well doing
here. if people be careful and if they be not careful they will not do
more good here over at home only money is easier earned here over
what it is at home and the only expensive thing here is clothes for
cloth of all kinds is double price and some things more and the only
thing easily purchased here is land and the produce of land sells very
well here and they raise good crops of wheat and barley…. But the
only drawback is the long winter for the frost comes on about the
middle of December and continues till about the first of May…. If

you please to send my black coat and britches as my father is served of them and they are no use to you being too small and they will be useful to some of my family. My family all seem to grow uncommonly fast for I do not think that you would know then already for the short time they have been out of your sight whether it is the climate or the change of food I do not know but it is very wholesome here."[2]

The first Scots, who settled on the Island from the late eighteenth century, laid the foundations for the subsequent waves of emigration which followed. Without them, the early Scottish domination of the Island would never have happened. Those who came to open up complete wilderness were true pioneers. It is one of life's great ironies that so many came from agriculturally restricted areas like Skye. But, while they may have been novices at tree felling and land clearance, Highlanders and Islanders proved themselves time and time again to have the staying power to endure the toughness and isolation of pioneer life. Their dogged determination to stay was matched by the enthusiasm shown by later groups to join forces with these early pioneers. From the 1790s to around 1810 large numbers flocked to Prince Edward Island from the northwest Highlands and Islands, with Skye, Mull and Colonsay being in the forefront of the movement. This all happened in spite of raging wars, escalating transport costs and viciously fought anti-emigration campaigns. If we add to this the anxieties felt by people who decide to leave their country and the countless real and imagined hazards of taking up the life of a new world settler, we are left gasping at the scale of the exodus from Scotland to the Island at this time.

In addition to considering the various forces operating in Scotland which may have influenced people to emigrate, a high priority has been placed on establishing the Island's pulling power to potential emigrants. The sudden rush of Scots during the Napoleonic War years happened just at the time when the Island's timber trade went through a steep rise. This drew ships regularly to the Island from the main Scottish ports, offering emigrants relatively inexpensive travel and the better settlement prospects which came from accelerating economic growth.

Tobermory Harbour in Mull c. 1888. Mull and Colonsay experienced large-scale emigration to the Island in the early 1800s. For many years Tobermory was the main embarkation port for Western Isle emigrants. *Copyright, George Washington Wilson Collection, Aberdeen University, D2207.*

The sudden entrance of Dumfriesshire emigrants to the Island from 1816 was due entirely to the effects of this trade. Opportunities to emigrate were immediately seized upon, as soon as and only when, shipping links became established between the port of Dumfries and the Maritimes. As the focus of the timber trade moved northward along the Northumberland Strait, so too did many of our emigrant Scots. Countless numbers of Scots relocated themselves in the Richibucto area of New Brunswick to be closer to the action. Thus, economic self-interest was and remained a compelling force in determining people's desire to emigrate and choice of location. We must remember too that the timber trade also gave emigrants the added bonus of better quality ships. The huge demand for shipping created scores of new ships. Shippers vied with each other to find human cargoes to fill their ship holds on westward bound journeys across the Atlantic. The popular imagery of cholera-ridden, unsafe shipping is completely unjustified.

We know from the records kept by the ship surveyors of the day that most emigrants travelled in decent, if not the best ships of the period.

However in considering why people emigrated when they did, we need to look beyond factors which pushed them from Scotland or the factors which pulled them to the Island. There is the wider world to consider. The first three contingents of Scots who left Perthshire, Argyll and west Inverness-shire in 1770 to settle on the Island made their move just six years before the signing of the American Declaration of Independence. The French Revolution would begin in just under twenty years. "Liberty" was acquiring its adherents as a new and powerful ideology, bringing with it radical notions of equality before the law and the political empowerment of ordinary people. An anonymous letter writer from Inverness expressed the new way of thinking in 1774. His letter found its way to the *Aberdeen Journal,* and offers various "motives for emigration to North America, as I had them from a body of Highlanders." They were all economically based except for the last one:

> "There are no titled proud lords to tyrannize over the lower sort of people, men being there [North America] upon a level, and more valued in proportion to their abilities than they are in Scotland."[3]

Although the northern colonies remained under British control they were quick to identify with American principles of "levelling down" and self-determination. Emigrants showed a healthy disregard for bureaucratic controls and British government edicts. Some of the wealthy proprietors who tried to establish settlers on the Island had high hopes of transposing their feudal ideas of land management to the Island but when they did, they were given short shrift by the ordinary colonisers. Scots slipped into the new way of thinking effortlessly. Predominating as they did in the early waves of emigration, they were some of the first to grapple with the maze of bureaucracy which constituted the Island's land tenure system. Their solution was simple. They worked out where they wanted to settle and squatted. There was

Charlotte Harbour by George Thresher, c. 1830, *courtesy of Prince Edward Island Public Archives and Records Office, Acc. 291611.*

no effective higher authority and land colonization proceeded more by the will of the people than by any grand plan of government.

Given this overall background, it is perhaps easier to see why the emigration movement engulfed so many areas of Scotland—especially the Highlands and Islands. With its relative closeness and accessible land, Prince Edward Island became the first to benefit. The Island maintained its sense of identity with the various regions of Scotland long after its initial colonisers had felled their first trees. The opponents of emigration never stood a chance in trying to hold back the exodus since they never came close to grasping the egalitarian and economic aspects of its appeal.

APPENDIX I

EXTANT PASSENGER LISTS FOR SHIP CROSSINGS FROM SCOTLAND TO P.E.I.

The eleven passenger lists recorded below are the only lists known to have survived for early ship crossings from Scotland to Prince Edward Island. Primary sources are recorded below but the transcripts themselves have been taken from the following secondary sources: Bigwood, "Two Lists of Intending Passengers to the New World 1770 and 1771" p. 22; Bumsted. *The Peoples Clearance*, pp. 232–33, 235–41, 265–80 and *The Island Magazine* No. 2 (1977) p. 41.

The lists vary in the amount and type of information they contain. Most of the early lists record emigrant locations in Scotland while the later ones do not. Ages were often recorded since fares were normally based on a sliding scale according to age.

(1) *Edinburgh* **of Campbeltown, John McMichael (master) from Campbeltown July, 1771** (SRO SC 54/2/106)
[Note: The list gives the fares paid by or on behalf of people travelling alone or as heads of households. It shows that ten sailed as cabin passengers and fifty-two travelled in the hold. However, the list does not necessarily cover all who sailed on this crossing but the small capacity of the brig (99 tons) would have greatly restricted the passenger numbers.]

Passenger name	By whom paid	Cabin	Hold	Rate(s)#	Total £	s	d
Hugh Montgomery	himself		5	70	17	10	
Neill Montgomery	Hugh Montgomery		1	70	4	1	9
Joseph McLean	Prov. Stewart*		1		3	10	
James Woodside	himself		2		7		
Janet Finlay	herself		1		3	10	
Alex McKay, sailor	himself		3		10	10	
Neill McKay for	himself		3		10	10	
Arch'd McKay	Neill McKay (his brother)		1		3	10	
John McVicar	himself		1		3	10	
Hector McShenoig	his father		1		3	10	
Dun. McWilliam	himself		4		14		
Dugd Campbell	in part per se		2		3		
Neill Shaw	himself as under		4		10	3	10
Neill McCallum	himself		4				
More McKay	indented		1				
Mrs Rob. Stewart	Prov. Stewart*	7	2	90			
Cap John Colvil	himself		7	70	21	10	
John McLarty	Prov. Stewart*		1	70	3	10	
John McGugan	Prov. Stewart*		2		7	10	

Passenger name	By whom paid	Cabin	Hold	Rate(s)#	Total £ s d
John McKay sen	Prov. Stewart*		2		
Archd McKenzie	Prov. Stewart*		2		
Dugald Stewart	Prov. Stewart*	2		90	
John McKay taylor	Prov. Stewart*		2	70	
Mr Craig	Prov. Stewart*	1		90	
Hector McEachine					
Neil McLeonan					
Andrew Wilson					
Peter McDougall					

* Provost Stewart is Peter Stewart who became a Chief Justice in PEI in 1775. He was a Campbeltown merchant and was part-owner of the *Edinburgh*.

Although there were exceptions, the standard fare for steerage was normally £3.10 (70s.) and cabin accommodation was normally £4.10 (90s.).

(2) *Lovelly Nelly,* **William Sheridan (master) from Whitehaven c. 1774** (PRO T 47/12)

Person's Name	Trade	Age	Place of residence	Parish	Reasons for leaving the country
John Smith	Blacksmith	33	Lachend	Colvend	Could not earn bread sufficient to support him and his family
Margrt McVicar		28			
Wm. & Mary Smith		6&5			
John McGeorge		24			
Jean Stevenson		66			
Jas. Wardrop	Mason	26	Haliaths	Lochmaben	Same reason
David Harrieson	Wheelwright	40	Ecclefechan	Hoddam	Same reason
Jannet Henderson		44			
Grizell Harrieson		19			
Agnes do		17			
Helen do		13			
Jannet & Margaret do		9&7			
John Crocket	Farmer	31	Thornyhill	Colvend	Same reason
Margt. Young		26			
Jas. Crocket		6			
Wm. & Jas. Crocket		4&1			
John McCracken		23			
Walwood Waugh	Joiner	33	Brownmoor	Annan	Same reason
Helen Henderson		30			
Four boys and one girl		from 10 to 1			
Cathn. Colven		30			
Margt. Campbell		26			
Wm. Campbell		24			
Wm. McKie	Mason	30	Cassaend	Kelton	Same reason
Issabel McKie		29			
John, Eliz. & Mary Mckie		6,4&1			
Wm. Troop	Mason	24	Do.	Do.	Same reason
John Troop	Labourer	22			
Alexr. Coupland	Do.	18			
Wm. McBurnie	Joiner	26	Fairgarth	Colvend	Same reason
Ro. McBurnie	Do.	20			
Barbra Henning					
Thos. Wm. & Christn. Armstrong	Labourers	17,15 &10	Nethermiln	Glencairn	Same reason
Chas. Blackie	Farmer	36	Milnbank	Southwick	Could not with all his industry support self & family

Person's Name	Trade	Age	Place of residence	Parish	Reasons for leaving the country
John Blackie		6			
Wm. Do.		4			
James Do.		3			
Ann Do.		10 mos.			
James Tyler	Wright	25			
Ro. Blair	Sailor	50	Drum	New Abbey	Same reason
Henry Shannen		20			
John Smith	Mason	45	Preston	Kirkbean	Same reason
Jant. Sturgeon					
Jant. Smith		6			
Mary Do.		9			
Agness Do.		5			
Issabela Do.		3			
Nelly Do.		1			
Ro. Coultart	Labourer	20	Lashmack-wharren	Kirkgunzeon	Same reason
Wm. Smith	Do.	24	Corsack	Colvend	Same reason
Mary Wilson		50			
Ro. Stewart	Do.	16	Knockhuley	Southwick	Same reason
Jannet Stewart		14			
Wm. Wilson	Labourer	23	Boreland	Colvend	Same reason
John Wilson	Do.	21	Do.	Do.	Same reason

(3) *Lovelly Nelly*, **William Sheridan (Master) from Dumfries, May 1775** (PRO T47/12)

Emigrant names	Ages	Occu-pations	Place of Residence	County	Quality	For what reason they leave Scotland
Thomas Henderson	32	Joiner	Hoddam	Annandale	Countryman	To seek better bread than he can get here
Margery Hoggs	32					
Martha his daughter	8					
Hanny do	4					
Thomas his son	1					
Joseph Graive	36	Weaver	New Abbey	Galloway	Countryman	The same reason as above
Marrion Buckley We	34					
John his son	10					
Robert do	8					
Mary his daughter	3					
Joseph Clark	45	Joiner	Sanquhar	Nithsdale	Countryman	To get better bread
Anne Wilkie wife	36					
Ann Clark daughter	4					
Joseph his son	15 mos.					
Robert Braiden	38	Labourer	Dumfries	Nithsdale	Countryman	To provide for his family a better livelihood
Jean Kirkpatrick We	26					
James his son	7					
William do 4) twins	4) twins					
David do	4)					
Edward do	7 mos.					
William Clark	30	Gardener	Caerlave-rock	do	do	do
Grizzoe Kissock wife	30					
John Clark child	10 mos.					
William Graham	25	Labourer	Dryfesdale	do	do	do

Emigrant names	Ages	Occu-pations	Place of Residence	County	Quality	For what reason they leave Scotland
Janet Rogerson	25					
James McCullock	48	Labourer	Dumfries	do	do	do
Jannet Johnston	60					
John Aitken	50	Labourer	Caerlaverock		do	do do
Margaret Lowdon We						
James his son	17					
Goddion do	7					
Margaret						
his daughter	4					
Agnes do	2					
James Douglas	57	Labourer	New Abbey	Galloway	do	To mend himself
Jannet Neish	53					
James his son	8					
Anthony Culton	30	Labourer	Troqueer	do	do	do
Jannet McCaughter	36					
Marrion his daughter	12					
Grizel do	7					
Jannet do	5					
Ann do	7 mos.					
Robert his son	10					
John do	4					
William Douglas	21	Labourer	Kirkbean	do	do	do
John Douglas	25	do	do			
James Gibson	45	Chapman		do	do	
Adam Gibson	31	Labourer	do	do		
David Irvine	37	Labourer	St. Mungo	Annandale	do	
Margaret Irvine	37					
William his son	11					
Jean a daughter	7					
James a son	3					
Robert Marshall	33	Weaver	Sanquhar	Galloway	do	To get a better employment
Elizabeth do	32					

Emigrant names	Ages	Occu-pations	Place of Residence	County	Quality	For what reason they leave Scotland
John his son	8					
Andrew do	4					
James do	4 mos					
Andrew Brigg	30	Black-smith	Kirkbean	Galloway	Countryman	To mend his Fortune
Margaret Griver	28					
John Carson	20	Labourer	Colvend	do	Countryman	To better himself
Charles Carson	18	do	do	do	do	do
Gavin Johnson	22	School-master	Bothwell	Lanark	Scholar	To get a place
William Blair	30	Mariner	Colvend	Galloway		For his health
Charles Aiken	22	Clerk	do	do		To look after the others
Thomas Chisholm	36	Farmer	Kirkbean	do		do

List of Families and Persons' Names received from Mr. Sheridan which is to embark at different places as under Viz.

Thomas Trumbell		Run away from this place
Jean Mackay his wife		
Trumbells 3 children	to be shipped at Douglas Isleman	
Robert Douglas		Run away
John Grinlaw	to be shipped at Whitehaven	do
Anthony McClilan		A man of good character
McClilans 5 children	to be shipped at Ballcarry Port Kirkcudbright	
John McClean		Good Character
His Wife	to be shipped at do Port Kirkcudbright	
His Son		

(4) *Jane*, **Fisher (Master) from Drimindarach July, 1790** [PANS MS File]

		Full Pass-engrs	12 to 8	8 to 6	6 to 4	4 to 2	under 2 yrs
			3/4 3/4	1/2 1/2	1/4 1/4	1/8 1/8	
Lodyvick M'Donald	Sauanistir, S. Morar, tenant	2					2
John MacDonald	Ardnafuaran	2		1	1		
Ranald M'Donald	Retland, S. Morar	2					1
Annabella M'Donald	Ardnafuaran, resident	1					
William Gillies	Tray, S. Morar, tenant	2					
John M'Gillvray	Mamy	6					
Angus M'Gillvray	Airnapoul	2		1		1	2
Lauchland M'Donald	Ardgasrig, resident	2					
William M'Gillvray	Mamy, tenant	3	1	1		2	1
Donald M'Eachen	Slockkardnish, tenant	2		2	1	1	1
John M'Donald	ditto, tenant	3	1	2	1		1
John MacDonald	ditto, tenant	1					
John Cambell	Island Shona, tenant	2					1
Donald Adamson	Pedlar, Moidart	2					
John MacGillvray jr	Mamy	2				1	1
Mary M'Donald	Ardnafuaran	1					
Marion M'Kinnon	Ardgasrig	1					
Ewen MacDonald	Retland, S. Morar, tenant	3		1	1		
Elexr. M'Kinnon	Ardgasrig	1					
Duncan Gillies	Duchaniss	4					
Donald Grant	Kenleod	5		1			
John MacDonald	Scamdale, S. Morar	5	1		1		
Hugh M'Gillvray	Arieniskill, tenant	2				1	2
Edmund Adamson	ditto, tenant	2					
Angus MacDonald	Drimindarach	3	1	1	1	2	1
Peter Gillies	Keppoch	2		1		1	1
Roderick M'Donald	Glenuis	2		1	1	1	1
Isabella M'Donald	Retland	1					
Keathrine M'Eachen	Airnapoul	1					
Alexander M'Donald	Torbey	2		1	1	1	1
John MacGillivray	Alisary, tenant	6					
Allan MacDonald	Lagan Ardnish, tenant	3	1				
James MacDonald	ditto, tenant	1					
Donald M'Donald	Fiorlindugh, tenant	1					
Donald M'Donald	Drimlaogh, taylor	3	1	1	1	1	2
Donald M'Donald	Kenchregain, tenant	2					
Keatherine M'Gillvray	Essan		1		1		
Donald M'Intyre	Ardgasrig	2				1	
Angus M'Cormick	Frebost, S. Uist	1					
Donald M'Cormick	ditto.	2				1	1
Hugh Morrison	Stoneybridge@	2		1	1		1

		Full Pass- engrs	12 to 8 3/4	8 to 6 1/2	6 to 4 1/4	4 to 2 1/8	under 2 yrs
John Walker	Askernish@	1					
Peter M'Innes	ditto	1					
John M'Innes	ditto	2				1	1
#John M'Phie	Frebost, resident	1					
Charles M'Lean	ditto	1					
Dugald M'Cormick	Gruilin, Isle of Eigg, pedlar		1				
Hugh M'Gillvray	Kyles, S. Morar	1					
Donald M'Donald	Isle of Eigg	2		1	2		1
John M'Donald	Fort William	2		1	1	1	
Donald M'Donald	Auberchaladair	3					1
Margery M'Donald	ditto	1					
Archibald Scott	ditto	2					
	Total number of passengers 111		6	16	13	17	23

@ in South Uist.
#Ann MacPhie in second List.

(5) *Lucy*, Robertson (Master) from Drimindarach July, 1790 [PANS MS File]

		Full Pass-engrs	12 to 8 3/4	8 to 6 1/2	6 to 4 1/4	4 to 2 1/8	under 2 yrs
Donald M'Donald	Isle Shona Moidart	3				1	1
Keathrine M'Isaac	Isle Shona Moidart	3					
Ann M'Donald	Isle Shona Moidart	2	2	1	1		1
Peggy M'Isaac	Isle Shona Moidart	1					
John M'Eachun	Isle Shona Moidart	2		1	1	1	
John M'Eachun	Isle Shona Moidart	1					
Donald M'Inrye	Kyles, Tenant	5	1	1		1	1
John MacPherson	Kyles, Tenant	3					
Donald M'Gillvray	Kyles, Carpenter	2					
Rodk. M'Donald	Kyles	2					
John M'Intyre	Kyles, Tenant	2					
Lauchlan Adamson	Glenuig, tenant	2				1	1
Alexander Adamson	Glenuig, tenant	4					
Alexander M'Donald	Glenuig, tenant	3		2		1	2
Alexander Corbet	carpenter portvat	1					
Johana M'Donald	Samlaman	1					
Donald M'Kellaig	Irin	1					
John M'Millan	Kenchregain, tenant	2					
Donald M'Millan	Kenchregain, tenant	2					1
John M'Eachun	Kenochailort	3	1	1		1	1
Angus M'Eachun	Arienskill, smith	4					2
Duncan M'Millan	Arienskill, tenant	2					1
Alexander M'Eachun	Arienskill, tenant	2					
Donald M'Donald	Arienskill, tenant	3					
Lauchlane M'Donald	Essan	3		1	2		
Mary M'Kellaig	Kyles S. Moror	2		1	1	1	1
Alexander M'Millan	Toray	2	1	1			
John M'Donald	Borrodale	4					
Alexander Chisholm	Kenleod	2				1	1
Alexander M'Donald	Galmistle, pedlar Isle of Eigg	6		1	1	1	
John M'Lean	Kildounain, tenant	5	1		1	1	
Angus M'Donald	Houlun Eigg	2				1	1
Donald M'Donald	Kentra Moidart	3				1	1
John M'Donald	Glenuig, tenant	2		2	1		1
Total number of passengers		**88**	**6**	**11**	**8**	**12**	**17**

(6) *Rambler* **of Leith, James Norris (Master) from Tobermory May, 1806** [PAPEI 2702]

No.	Males	above 60	from 16 to 60	under 16
1	James McLean		43	
2	Dond McLean		20	
3	Hugh McLean			14
4	Alexr McLean			6
5	Angus McLean			4
6	John Cameron		60	
7	Dond Cameron		30	
8	Alexr Cameron		20	
9	Allan Cameron			12
10	Angus Cameron			10 months
11	Dond Cameron			5
12	Dond Livingston		55	
13	Duncan Livingston		33	
14	John Livingston		30	
15	Alex Livingston			15
16	Duncan McLean		26	
17	Archd McLean		35	
18	Lauchn McLean			15
19	Duncan McLean			4
20	Lauchn McLean			6
21	Alexr Cameron		54	
22	Hugh Cameron		17	
23	John Cameron			15
24	Jas Cameron			5
25	Duncan Henderson		54	
26	Don Henderson			10
27	John Henderson			5
28	Archd Murray		21	
29	Alexr Cameron		28	
30	Angus McDonald		35	
31	Dond McDonald			13
32	John McDonald			11
33	Alexr McDonald			6
34	Neil Campbell		30	
35	Dond McInnis		38	
36	Angus McInnis			13
37	Angus McInnis		60	
38	Hector McInnis		30	
39	Allan McInnis		25	
40	Finlay McInnis			2
41	John McInnis			1

		above 60	from 16 to 60	under 16
42	John McLauchlan		50	
43	Duncan McLauchlin		21	
44	Colin McLauchlin		18	
45	Dond McLauchlin			16
46	Alexr McLauchlin			14
47	Jas McLauchlin			5
48	John Cameron		21	
49	Dond McLauchlin		30	
50	Dougald McLauchlin			6 months
51	John McArthur	78		
52	John McArthur		35	
53	John McArthur			3
54	John McEacharn		35	
55	Hector McEarchen			3
56	Allan McEarchen			2
57	Dond Livingston		25	
58	Malcolm Livingston			2 weeks
59	Geo. Norris McLean			2 days
60	Lauchlin McMillan		55	
61	Dond McMillan		25	
62	Hugh McMillan		18	
63	John McMillan			7
64	Hugh McPhee		36	
65	John McPhee		33	
66	John McNeil		25	
	Total	**1**	**35**	**30**

No.	Females	above 60	from 16 to 60	under 16
1	Peggy McLean		43	
2	Christian McLean		18	
3	Mary McLean			7
4	Ann Cameron		50	
5	Sarah Cameron		19	
6	Ann Cameron		17	
7	Flora Cameron			15
8	Mary Livingston		50	
9	Isabell Livingston		22	
10	Flora Livingston		17	
11	Cathe Livingston		22	
12	Margaret Livingston			1/2
13	Ann McLean		30	

		above 60	from 16 to 60	under 16
14	Ann McLean		34	
15	Mary McLean		25	
16	Maron McLean		19	
17	Mary McLean			3
18	Katrine McLean			4 months
19	Cathr Cameron		38	
20	Jean Cameron		20	
21	Jennet Cameron			14
22	Sarah Cameron			12
23	Cathe Cameron			2 months
24	Isabella Henderson		30	
25	Janet Henderson			8
26	Mary Henderson			3
27	Isabel Henderson			1
28	Mary Murray		48	
29	Margt Murray			13
30	Janet Murray			5
31	Mary Cameron		23	
32	Cathe Cameron			1
33	Mary McDonald		30	
34	Mary McDonald			9
35	Janet McDonald			7
36	Kathe McDonald			3
37	Ann McDonald			3 months
38	Janet Campbell		19	
39	Margeret McInnis		29	
40	Flora McInnis		25	
41	Mary McInnis			12
42	Sarah McInnis			8
43	Janet McInnis			6
44	Margt McInnis			3 months
45	Margt McInnis		50	
46	Mary McInnis		28	
47	Isabella McInnis			16
48	Ann McInnis			4 weeks
49	Christian McLauchlan		46	
50	Mary Cameron		50	
51	Mary McLauchlin		26	
52	Isabella McLauchlin			3
53	Mry McArthur		60	
54	Marion McArthur		25	
55	Cathe McArthur		30	
56	Mary McArthur		20	

		above 60	from 16 to 60	under 16
57	Cathe McArthur			10 months
58	Mary McEarchen		30	
59	Flora Livingston		24	
60	Sarah McMillan		50	
61	Margt McMillan		20	
62	Cathe McMillan			12
63	Sarah McPhee		20	
	Total		**36**	**27**

(7) *Humphreys* **of London, John Young (Master) from Tobermory June, 1806** [PAPEI 2702]

No.	Males	above 60	from 16 to 60	under 16
1	D'd McDonald		24	
2	Sam'l May Williams		32	
3	John Allen		25	
4	Tho's Allen			4
5	C.D.Rankin		29	
6	Geo. Rankin			3 months
7	Don'd McIntyre		23	
8	Gellin McPherson		38	
9	Arch'd McPherson			9
10	Arch'd McEarchern		30	
11	Lauchlin McEacher			3
12	John McEachern		22	
13	Lauchlin McDonald			11
14	Colin Connell		20	
15	Angus McDonald		60	
16	Don'd McDonald		20	
17	Don'd McEachern		60	
18	Don'd McEachern		24	
19	John Livingston		20	
20	Dugald McEarchen		18	
21	Hector McEarchen			9
22	Duncan Henderson		47	
23	Donald Henderson		18	
24	John Henderson			2
25	Hugh McKinnon		51	
26	Neal McKinnon		19	
27	John McKinnon			14
28	Malcolm McKinnon			12
29	Angus McKinnon			8
30	Rod'k McKinnon			2
31	Neal McKinnon		42	
32	Neal McKinnon		20	
33	Don'd McKinnon		26	
34	Alex'r McPhardon		28	
35	Angus McPhardon			2
36	Lauchlin McKinnon		45	
37	John McKinnon			4
38	Rod'k McKinnon			2
39	Duncan McKinnon			2 months
40	Angus McLane		55	

		above 60	from 16 to 60	under 16
41	John McLane		16	
42	Ja's McLane			14
43	Don'd McLane			10
44	Cha's McEachern		17	
45	Alex'r McQueary		40	
46	John McQueary			8
47	Sandy McQueary			6
	Total		27	20

No.	Females	above 60	from 16 to 60	under 16
1	Maria Williams		29	
2	Francis Allen		25	
3	Maria Allen			2
4	Flora Rankin		24	
5	Flora McIntyre		40	
6	Sarah McIntyre		20	
7	Mary McIntyre		18	
8	Flora McPherson		33	
9	Mary McPherso			4
10	Marg't McPherson			2
11	Jane McPherson			2 months
12	Sarah McEarchen		30	
13	Jane McEarchen			6
14	Marg't McEachern			1 month
15	Mary Carmichael		35	
16	Flora McDonald			9
17	Penny McDonald			7
18	Mary McDonald			4
19	Ann McDonald		50	
20	Cath'e McDonald		24	
21	Christ'n McDonald		22	
22	Sarah McEachern		52	
23	Mary McEarchen		19	
24	Jannet McEarchen			12
25	Sarah Henderson		47	
26	Mary Henderson		20	
27	Ann Henderson			14
28	Catherine McKinnon		45	
29	Mary McKinnon		20	

		above 60	from 16 to 60	under 16
30	Cath'e McKinnon			10
31	Elizabeth McKinnon			6
32	Cath'e McKinnon		40	
33	Ann McKinnon		18	
34	Miron McKinnon		25	
35	Mirron McKinnon			4
36	Cath'e McKinnon			1
37	Elizabeth McPhardon		24	
38	Cath'e McKinnon		38	
39	Marg McKinnon			8
40	Jennet McKinnon			6
41	Ann McLane		50	
42	Christy McLane		18	
43	Mary McLane			12
44	Ann McEacharn		50	
45	Isobele McQueary		33	
46	Flora McQueary			13
47	Sarah McQueary			11
48	Margaret McQueary			4
49	Una McQueary			1 month
	Total		27	22

(8) *Isle of Skye* **of Aberdeen, John Thom (Master) from Tobermory July, 1806** [PAPEI 2702]

No.	Males	above 60	from 16 to 60	under 16
1	Andrew McDonald		55	
2	Hugh McDonald			15
3	Ronald McDonald		35	
4	Don'd McNair		50	
5	Don'd McNair		20	
6	Rod'k McNair		22	
7	Angus McDonald		22	
8	Angus McEacharn	72		
9	Don'd McEacharn		40	
10	Angus McEacharn			13
11	Arch'd McEacharn			3
12	John McEacharn			2
13	Hugh McDonald		32	
14	Angus McDonald			1/2
15	Lauchlin McInnon			12
16	Hugh McDonald		23	
17	Alex'r Hunter		22	
18	Duncan Cameron			7
	Total	**1**	**10**	**7**

No.	Females	above 60	from 16 to 60	under 16
1	Janet McDonald		36	
2	Mary McDonald		34	
3	Mar't McDonald			5
4	Mary McDonald			2
5	Marrin McGilvray		40	
6	Ann McNair			16
7	Flora McNair			14
8	Marren McNair			9
9	Mary McGilvray		35	
10	Mary McEacharn		29	
11	CathrineMcEacharn			9
12	Jennet McDonald		23	
13	Betty McDonald			2
14	Mary McEacharn		37	

		above 60	from 16 to 60	under 16
15	Mary McEacharn		60	
16	Mary McDonald		20	
17	Mary McDonald		35	
18	Marg't Cameron			10
19	Mary Skinner		45	
	Total		**12**	**8**

(9) *Spencer* **of Newcastle, Forster Brown (Master) from Oban July, 1806** [PAPEI 2702]

No.	Males	above 60	from 16 to 60	under 16
1	Malcom McEacharn		58	
2	Don'd McEacharn		22	
3	Angus McEacharn			12
4	Angus McEacharn		32	
5	Neil McEacharn			7
6	James McEacharn			1 1/2
7	Dougald McNeil		60	
8	Alex'r McNeil		26	
9	Cha's McNeil			15
10	Dougald McNeil			12
11	Duncan Bell	78		
12	Dougald Bell		25	
13	Duncan Bell			7
14	Hector Campbell		30	
15	Neil Campbell			3
16	John Campbell			1
17	Malcolm McNeil		51	
18	John McNeil			14
19	James Currie		25	
20	James Currie			2
21	John Bell		40	
22	John Bell			3
23	Malcolm Bell	65		
24	Arch'd Bell		25	
25	Angus Bell		24	
26	Malcolm McWilliam		48	
27	Hector McMillan			13
28	James McMillan		19	
29	Alex'r McMillan			14
30	Malcolm McMillan			10
31	Duncan McMillan			4
32	Murdoch McMillan		55	
33	Duncan McDuff		54	
34	Dugald McDuff		17	
35	Don'd McDuff			2 1/2
36	Ja's Currie		30	
37	Duncan Munn		60	
38	Malcolm Munn		23	
39	Neil Munn		28	
40	Ja's Munn		20	
41	Angus Munn		31	

		above 60	from 16 to 60	under 16
42	Gilbert McAldridge		38	
43	John McAldridge			7
44	Alex'r McAldridge			5
45	Peter McAldridge			3
46	John McAldridge			1
47	Ja's Darroch		32	
48	Arch'd Darroch		20	
49	Don'd McNeil		34	
50	Malcolm McNeil			5
51	Don'd McNeil			2
52	Dougald McLean		32	
53	Allan McLean			6
54	Alex. McLean			2
55	Gilbert McLean			3 mos.
56	Hector McNeil		27	
57	Arch'd McEacharn		30	
58	Malcolm McEacharn			3
59	Angus Darroch		60	
60	Malcolm Darroch		20	
61	Duncan Darroch		28	
62	John Darroch			3
63	Don'd Shaw		30	
64	Peter McDougald		33	
	Total	**2**	**35**	**27**

		above 60	from 16 to 60	under 16
No.	**Females**			
1	Flora Buchanan		52	
2	Mary McEacharn		28	
3	Flora McMillan		51	
4	Isabella McNeil			7
5	Mary Bell		26	
6	Cath'e McEacharn		27	
7	Flora Bell			9
8	Christ'n McPhaden		27	
9	Mary Livingston		51	
10	Jannet McNeil		20	
11	Marg't Livingston		32	
12	Christian McDonald		36	
13	Mary Bell			15

		above 60	from 16 to 60	under 16
14	Nelly Bell			12
15	Catherine Bell			10
16	Janet Bell			5
17	Marg't Bell			1/2
18	Flora McDuffie		41	
19	Janet Bell		18	
20	Grissel McNeil		40	
21	Flora McMillan			8
22	Sophia McMillan			3 1/2
23	Cathrine McMillan			1
24	Mary McNeil		40	
25	Marg't McDuff		20	
26	Janet McDuff			14
27	Cathrine McDuff			9
28	Effy McDuff			5
29	Nancy McDuff		19	
30	Mary Currie			7 months
31	Flora Brown		58	
32	Ann Munn		17	
33	Effy Munn			15
34	Cathrine Currie		22	
35	Betty McMillan		18	
36	Marg't McNeil		21	
37	Cathrine Munn			7 months
38	Cath'e Darroch		30	
39	Janet Currie		55	
40	Rachel Darroch		37	
41	Marion Bell		34	
42	Mary McDuff	72		
43	Jane Currie		21	
44	Dolly Patterson	70		
45	Cathrine McLean		35	
46	Ann McEacharn		19	
47	Cath'e Currie		26	
48	Effy McAlester		60	
49	Nancy Brown		23	
50	Marg't McMillan		26	
51	Nancy Darroch		26	
	Total	**2**	**33**	**16**

(10) *Elizabeth and Ann* **of Newcastle, Thomas St. Girese (Master), from Thurso August, 1806**
[PAPEI 2702]

No.	Males	above 60	from 16 to 60	under 16
1	Geo. Loggan		58	
2	Jas. Loggan		23	
3	Geo. Loggan		20	
4	Rob't Loggan		18	
5	Walter Loggan			14
6	Alex'r Loggan			12
7	Will'm Loggan			16
8	Peter Loggan			8
9	Dougald Loggan			6
10	Norman McKay		36	
11	John McKay		47	
12	Murdoch McKay		19	
13	Hugh McKay			10
14	John McLeod		59	
15	Don'd McLeod		25	
16	Hugh McLeod			15
17	Angus McLeod			6
18	Kenneth McLeod		37	
19	John McLeod			12
20	Geo. McLeod			5
21	Kenneth McLeod			3
22	Jas. McLeod			1
23	John McLeod		35	
24	Hugh McLeod			10
25	Don'd McLeod			4
26	And'w McLeod			2
27	Hugh McLeod		36	
28	Hugh MCLeod			10
29	Don'd McKay		24	
30	Hugh McKay			1
31	Will'm McKay		40	
32	John McKay			16
33	Neil McKay			13
34	W'm McKay			12
35	Will'm McKay		58	
36	Kenneth McKay			15
37	Geo. McKay			14
38	Duncan McKay			13
39	Hugh McKay			7
40	John McKay			5

		above 60	from 16 to 60	under 16
41	Geo. Gordon		20	
42	Will'm McKay			2
43	Rob't Gunn		22	
44	Don'd Manson		21	
45	Henry Manson		18	
46	Jas. Sinclair		23	
47	Don'd Elder		21	
48	Jas. Sutherland		51	
49	Will'm Sutherland			8
50	Daniel Campbell		22	
51	Donald Bair		55	
52	John Bair			5
53	Jas. Bair		18	
54	Don'd Bair			16
55	Rob't Bair			14
56	Will'm Bair			10
57	Ja's McKenzie		22	
58	John McKenzie		21	
	Total		**27**	**31**

No.	Females	above 60	from 16 to 60	under 16
1	Christian Gair		51	
2	Jean Loggan		24	
3	Jean McKay			4
4	Ann McKay			2
5	Isabell McKay			1
6	Jean Murray		48	
7	Elizabeth McKay			16
8	Christian McKay			14
9	Marg't McKay			8
10	Ann McKenzie		50	
11	Barbara McLeod		18	
12	Neil McLeod			14
13	Wilelmina McLeod			9
14	Betsy McKay		30	
15	Nancy Morrison		30	
16	Marrion McLeod			10
17	Nancy McLeod			1

		above 60	from 16 to 60	under 16
18	Mary McPherson		32	
19	Isabel McLeod			12
20	Christian McLeod			8
21	Marion McKay		30	
22	Marg't McLeod			2
23	Cathrine McLeod			1
24	Ann McKay		24	
25	Christian McKay		39	
26	Janet McKay			6
27	Jean Scabie		50	
28	Jean McKay			12
29	Ann Campbell		26	
30	Isabel McKay		18	
31	Christian Ross		34	
32	Ann Sutherland		19	
33	Mary Sutherland			15
34	Janet Sutherland			12
35	Isabel Sutherland			3
36	Ann Sutherland			1
37	Janet Bair			7
38	Christian Bair			1
39	Marg't Sutherland		30	
	Total		**17**	**22**

(11) *Clarendon* **of Hull, James Hines (Master) from Oban Aug, 1808** [PRO CO 226/23]
[The first twenty names in the list were seamen and not emigrants. Each emigrant gave the
same reason when asked to state the 'Cause of Emigration'—'Want of employ.']

No.	Name	Agu	Occupation	Sex	Former Place of residence	County where from
21	Charles Gordon	22	Surgeon	Male	Edinburgh	Mid Lothian
22	James Hope Stewart	25	Supercargo	Male	Edinburgh	Mid Lothian
23	Jas. Robertson Junr.	32		Male	P.I.Island	Queens Co.
24	Jas. Robertson Senr.	79	Labourer	Male	Fortingall	Perth Co.
25	Catherine Robertson	71	His wife	Fem	Do.	Do.
26	Alex'r Robertson	37	Labourer	Male	Do.	Do.
27	Cathrine Robertson	31	His wife	Fem	Do.	Do.
28	Christian Moon	22	Spinster	Do.	Blair	Do.
29	Donald Stewart	24	Labourer	Male	Do.	Do.
30	Angus Cameron	40	Do.	Do.	Auchinleck	Ayr
31	Ann Cameron	27	his Wife	Fem	Do.	Do.
32	Mary Cameron	5	his D'r	Do.	Do.	Do.
33	Euphemia Cameron	3	Do.	Do.	Do.	Do.
34	John McGreigor	22	Labourer	Male	Strathgary	Perth
35	George Moon	27	Do.	Do.	Do.	Do.
36	Donald Dewer	22	Do.	Do.	Foss	Do.
37	Marg't Dewer	20	his Wife	Fem	Do.	Do.
38	Peter Mcfarlane	25	Labourer	Male	Caplia	Do.
39	Janet Mcfarlane	25	his Wife	Fem	Do.	Do.
40	John Gore	38	Labourer	Male	Strathbrand	Do.
41	Mungo Mcfarlane	28	Do.	Do.	Do.	Do.
42	Jas. Robertson	24	Do.	Do.	Do.	Do.
43	Duncan Robertson	21	Do.	Do.	Do.	Do.
44	William Scott	25	Do.	Do.	Do.	Do.
45	Thomas McGriegor	40	Do.	Do.	Aberfeldy	Do.
46	John McGriegor	12	Labourer	Male	Do.	Do.
47	Charles Stewart	14	Do.	Do.	Do.	Do.
48	Arch'd McGreigor	28	Do.	Do.	Appin	Do.
49	Christian McGreigor	24	his Wife	Fem	Do.	Do.
50	Alexr. McGreegor	3	Son	Male	Do.	Do.
51	Alexr. Anderson	36	Labourer	Do.	Fortingall	Do.
52	Isobel Anderson	32	his Wife	Fem	Do.	Do.
53	Jas. Anderson	10	his Son	Male	Do	Do.
54	Ann Anderson	8	his D'r	Fem	Do.	Do.
55	Christian Anderson	6	Do.	Do.	Do.	Do.
56	Isobel Anderson	4	Do.	Do.	Do.	Do.
57	John Kennedy	38	Labourer	Male	Foss	Do.
58	Janet Kennedy	30	his Wife	Fem	Do.	Do.
59	Janet Kennedy	8	his D'r	Do.	Do.	Do.

No.	Name	Age	Occupation	Sex	Former Place of residence	County where from
60	Donald Kennedy	6	his Son	Male	Do.	Do.
61	Eliz. Kennedy	4	his D'r	Fem	Do.	Do.
62	Dun. Kennedy	1	his Son	Male	Do.	Do.
63	James Donald	37	Labourer	Male	Athol	Do.
64	Isobel McDonald	35	his Wife	Fem	Do.	Do.
65	Donald McDonald	10	his Son	Male	Do.	Do..
66	Margt. McDonald	8	his D'r	Fem	Do.	Do.
67	Eliz. McDonal	4	Do.	Do.	Do.	Do.
68	John McDonald	2	Son	Male	Do.	Do.
69	Donald McDonald	27	Labourer	Male	Foss	Perth
70	Margt. McDonald	22	Wife	Fem	Do.	Do.
71	Eliz. McDonald	1	his D'r	Do.	Do.	Do.
72	Duncan Kennedy	25	Labourer	Male	Foss	Do.
73	Margt. Kennedy	22	his Wife	Fem	Do.	Do.
74	Jane Kennedy	1	his D'r	Do.	Do.	Do.
75	Donald Stewart	18	Labourer	Male	Athol	Do.
76	Donald Forbes	18	Do.	Do.	Foss	Do.
77	Joseph Kennedy	14	Do.	Do.	Do.	Do.
78	Peter Stewart	51	Do.	Do.	Athol	Do.
79	Ann Stewart	51	his Wife	Fem	Do.	Do.
80	Ann Stewart	16	his D'r	Do.	Do.	Do.
82	Niel Stewart	10	Do.	Do.	Do.	Do.
81	John Stewart	13	his son	Male	Do.	Do.
83	Donald Stewart	46	Labourer	Do.	Glencoe	Do.
88	Mary Stewart	1 1/2	Do.	Do.	Do.	Do.
84	Niel Stewart	35	Do.	Do.	Do.	Do.
85	Mary Stewart	27	his Wife	Fem	Do.	Do.
86	Christ'n Stewart	5	his D'r	Do.	Do.	Do.
87	Margt. Stewart	3	Do.	Do.	Do.	Do.
89	Christian Stewart	37	Sister	Do.	Do.	Do.
90	John Campbell	50	Labourer	Male	Rannoch	Do.
91	Cath. Campbell	45	his Wife	Fem	Do.	Do.
92	Cath. Campbell	20	his D'r	Do.	Do.	Do.
93	Margt. Campbell	18	Do.	Do.	Do.	Do.
94	Isobel Campbell	16	Do.	Do.	Do.	Do.
95	Mary Campbell	14	Do.	Do.	Do.	Do.
96	Janet Campbell	11	Do.	Do.	Do.	Do.
97	Eliz Campbell	9	his D'r	Fem	Ranock	Perth
98	Arch'd Campbell	4	Son	Male	Do.	Do.
99	Christn Campbell	1	D'r	Fem	Do.	Do.
100	Wm. McNaughton	28	Labourer	Male	Fortingall	Do.
101	Margt. McNaughton	17	his Wife	Fem	Do.	Do.
102	Donald McLean	18	Labourer	Male	Do.	Do.

No.	Name	Age	Occupation	Sex	Former Place of residence	County where from
103	Chas. McLean	22	Do.	Do.	Do.	Do.
104	Mary McLean	21	his Wife	Fem.	Do.	Do.
105	Christian McLean	1	his d'r	Do.	Do.	Do.
106	Jane McLean	20	sister	Do.	Do.	Do.
107	Janet Brodie	30	Spinster	Do.	Glasgow	Lanark
108	George Brodie	4	son	Male	Do.	Do.
109	Hugh McNeil	21	Labourer	Do.	Mull	Argyll
110	John McNeil	17	Do.	Do.	Do.	Do.
111	Hector McQuarrie	23	Do.	Do.	Do.	Do.
112	Lach'n McQuarrie	21	Do.	Do.	Do.	Do.
113	Margt. McQuarrie	60	Spinster	Fem	Do.	Do.
114	Niel McCallum	32	Lbourer	Male	Do.	Do.
115	Mary McCallum	32	his Wife	Fem	Do.	Do.
116	John McCallum	12	Son	Male	Do.	Do.
117	Finlay McCallum	5	Do.]twins	Do.	Do.	Do.
118	Arch. McCallum	5	Do.]	Do.	Do.	Do.
119	Mary McCallum	3	daughter	Fem	Do.	Do.
120	Donald McCallum	1	Son	Male	Do.	Do.
121	Donald McDonald	32	Labourer	Do.	Do	Do.
122	Ann McDonald	25	his Wife	Fem	Mull	Do.
123	Cath. McDonald	3	Daughter	Do.	Do.	Do.
124	Malcolm McDonald	1	Son	Male	Do.	Do.
125	Janet McDonald	57	Mother	Fem	Do.	Do.
126	Cath. McDonald	26	Sister	Do.	Do.	Do.
127	Lauch'n McLean	60	Labourer	Male	Do.	Do.
128	Cath. McLean	56	his Wife	Fem	Do.	Do.
129	Flora McLean	30	his D'r	Do.	Do.	Do.
130	Hugh McLean	25	Son	Male	Do.	Do.
131	Ann McLean	20	D'r	Fem	Do.	Do.
132	Hector McLean	15	Son	Male	Do.	Do.
133	John McLean	12	Do.	Do.	Do.	Do.
134	Euphemia McLean	10	Daughter	Fem	Do.	Do.
135	John Campbell	56	Labourer	Male	Do.	Do.
136	Isobel Campbell	56	his Wife	Fem	Do.	Do.
137	Roderick Campbell	30	Son	Male	Do.	Do.
138	Donald Campbell	25	Do.	Do.	Do.	Do.
139	Alan Campbell	9	Do.	Do.	Do.	Do.
140	Patk. Ferguson	40	Labourer	Do.	Do.	Do.
141	Allan McLean	38	Do.	Do.	Do.	Do.
142	Angus McLean	60	Do.	Do.	Do.	Do.
143	Mary McLean	26	Daughter	Fem	Do.	Do.
144	Ann McLean	25	Do.	Do.	Do.	Do.
145	John McGiloray	3	Grandson	Male	Do.	Do.

No.	Name	Age	Occupation	Sex	Former Place of residence	County where from
146	Donald McKinnon	34	Labourer	Male	Do.	Do.
147	Mary McKinnon	22	his Wife	Fem	Do.	Do.
148	Allan McKinnon	24	his brother	Male	Mull	Do.
149	Cath. McKinnon	20	Sister	Fem	Do.	Do.
150	Cath. McKinnon	2	his D'r	Do.	Do.	Do.
151	Lach McLean	25	Labourer	Male	Do.	Do.
152	Ann McLean	30	his Wife	Fem	Do.	Do.
153	Janet McLean	1/2	Daughter	Do.	Do.	Do.
154	John Munn	48	Labourer	Male	Colonsay	Do.
155	Cathn Munn	42	Wife	Fem	Do.	Do.
156	Donald Munn	16	his Son	Male	Do.	Do.
157	Duncan Munn	14	Do.	Do.	Do.	Do.
158	Sarah Munn	12	his Daughter	Fem	Do.	Do.
159	Cathn Munn	7	Do.	Do.	Do.	Do.
160	Barbara Munn	5	Do.	Do.	Do.	Do.
161	John Munn	4	Son	Male	Do.	Do.
162	Sarah McLean	24	Spinster	Fem	Mull	Do.
163	Donald Campbell	26	Labourer	Male	Do.	Do.
164	Ann Campbell	23	his Wife	Fem	Do.	Do.
165	Charles McLean	21	Labourer	Male	Do.	Do.
166	Archd. McKinnon	18	Do.	Do.	Do.	Do.
167	Margt. McKinnon	40	his Mother	Fem	Do.	Do.
168	Mary McKinnon	12	Sister	Do.	Do.	Do.
169	John McEachran	30	Labourer	Male	Do.	Do.
170	Margt. McEachran	35	his Wife	Fem	Do.	Do.
171	Hugh McEachran	10	his Son	Male	Do.	Do.
172	Alexr McEachran	7	Do.	Do.	Do.	Do.
173	Janet McEachran	5	his Daughter	Fem	Do.	Do.
174	Cath. Lamont	14	Step D'r	Fem	Mull	Do.
175	Euphemia McKinnen	40	Spinster	Do.	Do.	Do.
176	Niel McKinnen	55	Farmer	Male	Do.	Do.
177	Margt. McLean	50	Wife	Fem	Do.	Do.
178	John McLean	22	Son	Male	Do.	Do.
179	Cath McLean	20	D'r	Fem	Do.	Do.
180	Margt. McLean	10	Do.	Do.	Do.	Do.
181	Niel McNiel	38	Labourer	Male	Do.	Do.
182	Ann McNiel	38	Wife	Fem	Do.	Do.
183	Torquil McNiel	13	Son	Male	Do.	Do.
184	Mary McNiel	10	D'r	Fem	Do.	Do.
185	John McNiel	8	Son	Male	Do.	Do.
186	Duncan McNiel	6	Son	Male	Mull	Argyll
187	Cath McNiel	4	his D'r	Fem	Do.	Do.
188	Sarah McKinnon	4[?]	Spinster	Do.	Do.	Do.

No.	Name	Age	Occupation	Sex	Former Place of residence	County where from
189	Hector McKinnon	21	Labourer	Male	Do.	Do.
190	Malcolm McKinnon	17	his brother	Do.	Do.	Do.
191	Dun McKinnon	31	Labourer	Do.	Do.	Do.
192	Julia McKinnon	28	his Wife	Fem	Do.	Do.
193	Mary McKinnon	24	his Sister	Do.	Do.	Do.
194	Margt. McKinnon	22	Do.	Do.	Do.	Do.
195	Cath McKinnon	21	Do.	Do.	Do.	Do.
196	Alexr. McDonald	21	Labourer	Male	Do.	Do.
197	Finlay McKinnon	26	Labourer	Do.	Do.	Do.
198	Mary McKinnon	23	his Wife	Fem	Do.	Do.
199	Allan McKinnon	3	Son	Male	Do.	Do.
200	Euphemia McKinnon	2	Daughter	Fem	Do.	Do.
201	Alexr. Campbell	22	Labourer	Male	Do.	Do.
202	Mary Campbell	24	Sister	Fem	Do.	Do.
203	Sarah Campbell	27	Do.	Do.	Do.	Do.
204	Malcolm McKinnon	24	Labourer	Male	Do.	Do.
205	Margt. McKinnon	50	his Mother	Fem	Do.	Do.
206	Lauch McKinnon	20	his brother	Male	Do.	Do.
207	Hector McKinnon	16	Do.	Do.	Do.	Do.
208	John McKinnon	14	Do.	Do.	Do.	Do.

APPENDIX 11

EMIGRANT SHIP CROSSINGS FROM SCOTLAND TO P.E.I., 1770–1850

Explanatory Notes

a) Passenger Numbers are taken from a number of sources, which sometimes give conflicting information. At best they are approximations and in some cases are highly ambiguous. We cannot be certain whether totals refer to adults only, just male heads of households, or include entire families (i.e. all children). Some ships made several stops to disembark passengers, so we cannot be sure which numbers relate to Prince Edward Island arrivals. For instance, with most sailings from Dumfries, the stated passenger numbers are an amalgam of the numbers bound for ports in New Brunswick as well as the Island. Where ships are known to have carried unspecified numbers of passengers, this is noted by a "?"

b) Vessel Details are taken from the *Lloyd's Shipping Register* and record:

i) **Vessel Type**:

Sailing Ship Rigs were many and varied. A major differentiation was the alignment of the sails. There were the Square Rig ships in which the sails were rigged across the ship and the Fore-and-Aft Rigs which followed the fore-and-aft line of the ship.

The Square Rig was normally used on ocean-going vessels. The Brig, a two-masted vessel with square rigging on both masts, was a very old and efficient design. Snows were commonly the largest type of two-masted rig and were fully square-rigged on both main masts. The Barque, usually a three-masted vessel, had its main masts square rigged (usually two) and the rear mast fore-and-aft-rigged. A full-rigged Ship was square-rigged on all masts (at least 3 masts).

The Schooner was a Fore-and-Aft Rigged ship with two or more masts while the Sloop had only one-mast. Fore-and-Aft rigged ships were normally used in the fishing and coastal trade.

ii) **Registered Tonnage**

A standard measure used to determine customs dues and navigation fees.

iii) **Place Where Vessel was built and in which Year**

When a ship was captured and acquired as result of naval warfare, it was called a Prize.

iv) *Lloyd's Shipping Register* **Code**

The codes, assigned after periodic surveys, refer to the quality, condition and age of ships:

A   first class condition and within a prescribed age limit at the time of sailing;

AE (from 1835)—"the second description of the first class," fit, no defects but over a prescribed age limit;

E   (before 1835)—second class, perfect repair, no defects;

E   (from 1835)—second class, unfit for carrying dry cargoes but safe for long sea voyages;

I   third class, only suitable for short voyages (i.e. not out of Europe);

O   (before 1835)—fourth class, out of repair, not safe or sea-worthy

The above letters were followed by the number 1 or 2 which signified the condition of the vessel's equipment. Where satisfactory, the number 1 was used, and where not, 2 was used.

Vessel Name Departure Port	Captain Emigrant Geographical Origins	Departure Year Month	Arrival Month P.E.I. Location (if known)	Passenger Nos.
Falmouth Greenock	McWhae, John Mainly Perthshire	1770 April	June Stanhope (Lot 34).	60 Psgrs

MacEwan, "The *Falmouth* Passengers," pp.12–19; Adams and Somerville, *Cargoes of Despair and Hope.* pp. 54–5; Malpeque Historical Society, *Malpeque and its People.* pp. 22–7.
The group was taken to Lord Advocate James Montgomery's township at Stanhope. He employed David Lawson, an experienced flax farmer to run his plantation, using emigrants as indentured servants. The *Falmouth* passengers were recruited by Lawson and many shared his Perthshire origins.

| *Annabella* Campbeltown | Stewart, Dugald Argyll | 1770 July | Sept Malpeque (Lot 18) | 100 Psgrs |

Lawson, "Early Scottish Settlement on Prince Edward Island: The Princetown Pioneers, 1769–1771," pp. 112–30; *SM*, vol. xxxiii (1771) p.379.
Lt. Col. Robert Stewart, who purchased half of Lot 18, recruited many emigrants from his native Argyll. Another Robert Stewart (Robert's brother-in-law) travelled on the *Annabella* and organised the initial settlement. Some settlers later left Malpeque and moved to Low Point (Lot 13) on the west side of Malpeque Bay, where there had been an Acadian settlement.

| *Edinburgh* of Campbeltown Campbeltown | McMichael, John Argyll | 1771 July | Malpeque (Lot 18) | 100 Psgrs |

Passenger List (Partial): *SRO SC* 54/2/106.
Bigwood, "Two Lists of Intending Passengers to the New World, 1770 and 1771," pp.17–22; Malpeque Historical Society, *Malpeque and its People.* pp. 21, 319.
Vessel Details: Brig, 79 tns., built 1765 Leith.
Sources differ but it is likely that at least 70 emigrants travelled on the *Edinburgh*; some families had their fares paid by Provost (Peter) Stewart, a Campbeltown merchant who became Chief Justice of PEI in 1775. Given the Stewart's ownership of Lot 18, it is probable that the group initially settled in the Malpeque Bay area.

| *Alexander* Arisaig and Lochboisdale | Kirkwood, J. South Uist, Barra, Eigg & mainland West Invernesshire | 1772 March | June Scotchfort (Lot 36) | 214 Psgrs |

Lawson, "Passengers on the *Alexander*', pp.127–43; Bumsted, *The People's Clearance.* pp.57–61.
The group, all Roman Catholics, was led by John MacDonald of Glenaladale, a Clanranald tacksman. They settled at Lot 36 on land purchased from Lord Advocate James Montgomery. Many of the mainland emigrants originated from Moidart and Knoydart. John MacDonald chartered the brig *Alexander* from John Buchanan & Co. of Greenock.

Vessel Name Departure Port	Captain Emigrant Geographical Origins	Departure Year Month	Arrival Month P.E.I. Location (if known)	Passenger Nos.
Lovelly Nelly Whitehaven	Sheridan, William Kirkcudbrightshire & Dumfriesshire	1774	N/K	67 Psgrs

Passenger List: *PRO* T 47/12
Vessel Details: Brig, 150 tns., built 1731, Britain; I2
The passenger list is undated but almost certainly refers to a 1774 crossing. Many of the emigrants later moved on to Pictou. The group included 4 masons, 1 blacksmith, 2 wheelwrights, 2 farmers, 3 joiners, 9 labourers and 1 sailor. The Captain's name is given as William Sherwin in the *Lloyds Shipping Register*. The *Lovelly Nelly* had been assigned an 'I' shipping code, signifying that the brig's hull was in poor condition.

Lovelly Nelly Dumfries	Sheridan, William Dumfriesshire, Kirkcudbrightshire & Peebleshire	1775 May	N/K	82 Psgrs

Passenger List: *PRO* T 47/12
Vessel Details: See above
The group included 2 joiners, 2 weavers, 12 labourers, 1 gardener, 1 chapman (pedlar), 1 blacksmith, 1 school master, 1 mariner, 1 clerk and 1 farmer.

John and Elizabeth	Morayshire	1775 June (Est.)	Orwell Bay (Lot 57)	52 Psgrs

PAPEI Acc 2779/1; Adams and Somerville, *Cargoes of Despair and Hope.* p. 61; PEI Gen. Soc. *Survey, Newspapers*, p. 8.
Seven families intended to settle at Lot 57, acquired in 1767 by Samuel Smith, a merchant, but they left without trace. It is thought that the settlement failed because of inadequate provisioning and its remote location. The group included William Simpson, and his wife, Janet Winchester. Helen Simpson, from Morayshire, wife of William Clark is also likely to have sailed on the *John and Elizabeth*.

Elizabeth London	Argyll	1775 Aug	Stanhope (Lot 34).	14 Psgrs

Jones and Fraser, "Those Elusive Immigrants" (Part 3), p.30; Adams and Somerville, *Cargoes of Despair and Hope.* pp.59–60.
The passengers boarded ship at Cork. They included Chief Justice Peter Stewart's family and servants (Peter was brother of Robert Stewart, proprietor of half of Lot 18). Peter Stewart leased part of Lot 34 from Sir James Montgomery. He had expected that a large number of single men would wish to go to PEI with him, but alarming news of an impending war discouraged most from emigrating.

Vessel Name Departure Port	Captain Emigrant Geographical Origins	Departure Year	Month	Arrival Month P.E.I. Location (if known)	Passenger Nos.

Jane
Drimindarach

Fisher

North and South Morar, Moidart,
Eigg and South Uist

1790   July   Aug.   186 Psgrs
                                    Lots 37 to 39

Passenger List: *PANS MS File* and *SCA (Oban Papers)*.
Lawson, *"Lucy, Jane and the Bishop,"* pp.1–13; Adams and Somerville, Ibid, pp.191–92. Harvey, *Journeys to the Island*, pp.76–7.
The *Jane* and *Lucy* sailed in convoy. The passengers were from the Clanranald estate and most had Catholic affiliations. One hundred and eleven of the 186 passengers were adults. The *British Queen* sailed in the same convoy but she took her passengers on to Quebec.

Lucy
Drimindarach

Robertson

North and South Morar, Moidart,
Eigg and South Uist

1790   July   Aug.   142 Psgrs
                                    Lots 37 to 39

Passenger List: *PANS MS File*. and *SCA (Oban Papers)*.
Vessel Details: Ship, 133 tns., built 1781; E1.
All were from the Clanranald estate and most were Roman Catholics. The *Lucy* carried 88 adults.

Mally of Greenock
Greenock

Maxwell, John

Uist

1791   June   Sept.   236 Psgrs
                                    Lots 37 to 39

NLS Adv.MS.73.2.13; *PAPEI* RG9 (Customs); *SRO* E504/15/59; *PEIRG* 9 Sept. 1791.
Vessel Details: Brig, 148 tns., built 1784 Greenock; A1.
The *Mally* carried 174 "full passengers" (i.e. adult). She left Greenock with 30 passengers and the remainder were probably collected from Uist. According to The *Royal Gazette* the *Mally* "was without fuel part of passage and her water was so bad that it was scarcely possible to use it." The *Mally* was due to sail on to North Carolina.

Queen of Greenock
Greenock

Morison, William

Uist

1791   June   Sept.   300 Psgrs
                                    Lots 37 to 39

As for *Mally* above.
Vessel Details: Brig, 200 tns., built 1782 Hull; A1.
The *Royal Gazette* stated that the *Queen* arrived with 300 passengers who spoke "handsomely of the kind treatment they received from Capt. Morison; his conduct is worthy of being followed by all masters of vessels and humanity should dictate a similar treatment." She carried 240 "full passengers." Forty passengers left from Greenock and the remainder were almost certainly collected from Uist. The *Queen* was due to sail on to North Carolina.

Argyle
Glenelg from
Greenock

Glen Garry, Inverness-shire

1793   150 Psgrs

Jones and Fraser, 'Those Elusive Immigrants' (Part 1), p.37.

Vessel Name Departure Port	Captain Emigrant Geographical Origins	Departure Year Month	Arrival Month P.E.I. Location (if known)	Passenger Nos.

Vessel Details: Brig, 139 tns., built 1790 Nova Scotia; A1
This group from Inverness-shire was en route to Glengarry County in Upper Canada. They were delayed by bad weather spending the winter of 1793 in P.E.I. They reached their final destination the following year.

Mennie Port Glasgow	McKellar, Daniel Uist	1802 June	Aug. N/K	274 Psgrs

SRO RH 4/188/1,2 vol. iii pp.531–35; Jones and Fraser, "Those Elusive Immigrants" (Part 1), p. 37.
Vessel Details: Ship, 274 tns. built 1802 New Brunswick; A1.
After leaving Port Glasgow, the *Mennie* almost certainly collected her passengers in Uist. Passenger baggage is recorded in the P.E.I. customs records but numbers are not given. The passenger total of 274 is taken from the *Highland Society of Scotland*'s records, which show that the *Mennie* had been fitted out at Port Glasgow to take passengers from the Western Isles to America.

Bess Tobermory		1803	N/K	80 Psgrs

Telford, Thomas, *A Survey and Report of the Coasts and Central Highlands of Scotland*: Second Appendix to the First Report (London, 1803).
The *Bess* was in a list of vessels with more than 30 passengers, which were preparing to clear out in 1803, and her destination was P.E.I.

Oughton Uist from Greenock	Baird, J. Mainly Uist	1803 June	Aug. Belfast (Lot 57)	200 Psgrs

SRO CS 96/1238; PAPEI RG9; GC 9 April, 1803, GH 24 June, 1803; White, *Lord Selkirk's Diary 1803–04.* pp. 4, 6, 35; Telford, *Survey of the Highlands, 1803.* Adams and Somerville, *Cargoes of Despair and Hope.* pp. 197, 222.
Vessel Details: Brig, 207 tns., built 1787 Leith; E2.
One of three ships (*Dykes, Oughton* and *Polly*) which took 800 people from Uist and Skye as well as from Wester Ross and Argyll to the Selkirk settlements at Belfast. The *Oughton* sailed on to Quebec to collect a cargo of wheat and timber before returning to Scotland.

Dykes Tobermory from Liverpool	Thompson, John Mainly Skye	1803 June	Aug. Belfast (Lot 57)	200 Psgrs

As for the *Oughton* above.
Vessel Details: Snow, 235 tns., built 1798 Maryport; A1.
Selkirk himself sailed on the *Dykes.* Her captain owned her at the time.

Polly Skye from Greenock	Darby, Thomas Mainly Skye	1803 June	Aug. Belfast (Lot 57)	400 Psgrs

As for the *Oughton* above.

Vessel Name Departure Port	Captain Emigrant Geographical Origins	Departure Year Month	Arrival Month P.E.I. Location (if known)	Passenger Nos.

Vessel Details: Ship, 284 tns., built 1762 Whitby; E1.
The *Polly*, owned by her captain, took 280 "full passengers" or 400 persons to Belfast. According to Thomas Telford's survey of 1803 the *Polly* was due to go on to New Brunswick. Selkirk apparently advertised for his ships. The *Glasgow Courier* stated that a ship was required to carry 400 passengers from Skye to P.E.I. or Pictou, Nova Scotia. The berths for each person were to be 6 ft by 18 inches and there was to be an allowance of 56 gallons of water and 2 barrels bulk of storage for each person besides sufficient room to be left in the hold for provisions.

Nancy	Church, W.S.	1805 May (Est.)	June	32 Psgrs
Tobermory	West Highlands & Islands		N/K	

PAPEI RG9; GA 12 March 1805; Harvey, *Journeys to the Island*. pp.76–77.
The *Greenock Advertiser* stated: "for freight or charter to Halifax, New Brunswick, Pictou or Newfoundland; The schooner *Nancy*…would engage to carry out a load of passengers. Alan Ker & Co." The passengers were landed at Three Rivers.

Northern Friends	McPherson, Archibald	1805 Aug (Est.)	Oct.	91 Psgrs
of Clyde				
Stornoway	Outer Hebrides & Wester Ross		Flat River (Lot 60)	

PAPEI RG9; Brehaut, Mary C., "Early Immigration (from the United Kingdom) to P.E.I. 1769–1878," *Lloyds List*.
Vessel Details: Ship, 245 tns., Prize, built 1790 Finland; E1.
The ship carried a group led by Kenneth McKenzie of Ross-shire. She returned to the Clyde in Dec. 1805 with a cargo of timber.

Rambler of Leith	Norris, James	1806 May	June	130 Psgrs
Tobermory	West Highlands & Islands—esp. Mull & Colonsay		Some to Lots 62 & 65	

Passenger List*: PAPEI 2702.*
SRO E504/35/1; Lloyds List.
Vessel Details: Brig, 296 tns., built 1800 Leith; A1.
The *Rambler* returned to Leith from Pictou with a timber cargo in October. Passenger baggage: 77 chests, 41 bussels, 24 bags, 10 bundles, 3 trunks, bed clothing and wearing apparel.

Humphreys	Young, John	1806 June	July	97 Psgrs
of London				
Tobermory	West Highlands and Islands—esp. Mull & Colonsay		Some to Lots 62 & 65	

Vessel Name	Captain	Departure		Arrival	Passenger
Departure Port	Emigrant Geographical Origins	Year	Month	Month	Nos.
				P.E.I. Location (if known)	

Passenger List: *PAPEI 2702*.
SRO E504/35/1; Lloyd's List.
Vessels Details: Ship, 250 tns., built 1785 Stockton; E1.
Passenger baggage: 42 chests, 23 barrels, 10 bags, 2 bundles, 17 beds, 7 trunks, 4 bags of used wearing apparel, beds and bed clothing.

Isle of Skye	Thom, John	1806	July	Sept.	37 Psgrs
of Aberdeen	West Highlands				
Tobermory	& Islands—esp.			Some to Lots	
	Mull & Colonsay			62 & 65	

Passenger List: *PAPEI 2702*.
SRO E504/35/1; PAPEI RG9.
Vessel Details: Snow, 181 tns., built 1806 Aberdeen; A1.
Passenger baggage: 22 chests, 5 trunks, 7 parcels, 13 casks containing used wearing apparel and bed clothes.

| *Pallas* | Robinson | 1806 | July | | ? Psgrs |
| Greenock | | | | N/K | |

GA 11 June, 1806; *QM* 24 Sept., 1806.
Vessel Details: Ship, 632 tns., built 1802 Prussia; A1.
Pallas bound for Quebec. The *Greenock Advertiser* stated "If sufficient numbers of passengers offer, the *Pallas* will be able to call at a port in the Highlands to take them on board and will land them at the Island of Saint John, Sydney, Pictou or any other convenient port in the Gulf of St. Lawrence as they may incline."

Spencer of Newcastle	Brown, Forster	1806	July	Sept.	114 Psgrs
Oban	West Highlands			Some to Lot 65	
	& Islands—esp.				
	Mull & Colonsay				

Passenger List: *PAPEI 2702*.
SRO E504/25/3.
Vessel Details: Ship, 330 tns., built 1778 Shields; E1.
Passenger Baggage: 72 chests, 4 trunks, 35 barrels, 8 boxes, 1 hogshead, 1 kettle, 40 parcels, wearing apparel/bedding.

Elizabeth and Ann	St Girese, Thomas	1806	Aug		107 Psgrs
of North Shields					
Thurso	North East Highlands—some			Lots 20 and 21	
	Durness & Tongue				

Vessel Name Departure Port	Captain Emigrant Geographical Origins	Departure Year	Month	Arrival Month	Passenger Nos. P.E.I. Location (if known)

Passenger List: *PAPEI 2702*.
GA 13 August 1806; *SRO E504/7/5*.
Vessels Details: 286 tns.
According to the *Greenock Advertiser* the *Elizabeth and Ann* was destined for Pictou.

Rebecca and Sarah of Leith Tobermory	Condee, James West Highlands & Islands—esp. Mull & Colonsay	1806	Sept		118 Psgrs Some to Lots 62 and 65

SRO E504/35/1.
Vessel Details: 284 tns., built 1778, Dutch Prize; E1.
Passenger baggage: 72 chests, 6 trunks, 36 barrels containing wearing apparel and clothing.

Elizabeth Oban	Milne, William West Highlands & Islands—esp. Mull, Colonsay	1808	July (Est.)	Aug.	96 Psgrs Some to Lot 65

PAPEI RG9.
Vessel Details: Ship, 214 tns., built 1789 Greenock; E1.

Mars Oban	Caithness, George West Highlands & Islands—esp. Mull and Colonsay	1808	July (Est.)	Sept.	94 Psgrs Some to Lot 65

PAPEI RG9.
Vessel Details: Snow, 208 tns., built 1806 Sunderland; A1.

Clarendon of Hull Oban	Hines, James Mainly Perthshire (Fortingall, Rannoch & Athol) & Argyll (esp. Mull)	1808	Aug	Sept.	208 Psgrs Some to Lots 47 & 52

Passenger List: *PRO CO 226/23*.
Vessel Details: Ship, 416 tns., built 1783 Bristol; E1.
The passengers consisted of 188 settlers and 20 crew. Some of the emigrants established New Perth (Lot 52).

Albion Dundee	Kidd, R.	1809	May	June N/K	39 Psgrs

Jones and Fraser, "Those Elusive Immigrants" (Part 1), p. 37; *QG* 6 July 1809.

Vessel Name Departure Port	Captain Emigrant Geographical Origins	Departure Year Month	Arrival Month P.E.I. Location (if known)	Passenger Nos.

Vessel Details: Brig, 152 tns, built Dysart 1805, A1.
A further 60 passengers sailed on to Quebec on the *Albion* arriving in early July.

Catherine of Leith Tobermory?	West Highlands & Islands—esp. Mull	1810	Mainly Lots 30 and 65	? Psgrs

MacDonald, Colin S. 'Early Highland Emigration to Nova Scotia and Prince Edward Island from 1770-1853', *Nova Scotia Historical Society (collections)* vol. xxiii (1936) pp. 41–8.

Phoenix Tobermory	West Highlands and Islands—esp. Mull	1810	Mainly Lots 30 and 65	? Psgrs

As for *Catherine* of Leith above.

Neptune of Ayr Greenock	Neil, J	1811 April	June N/K	? Psgrs

SRO CS 96/4475; *QG* 6 June, 1811p; Jones and Fraser, "Those Elusive Immigrants" (Part1), p. 37.
Vessel Details: Brig, 167 tns., built 1799 Ayr; E1.
Major Drummond of the 104th Regiment left at Charlottetown.

Curlew Greenock	Young, John Perthshire: mainly Dull, Killin and Comri	1818 July	Upper Canada but some settled in PEI	205 Psgrs

Passenger List: *PRO CO 384/3*.   *PRO CO 226/36*.
Vessel Details: Brig, 260 tns., built 1815 Newcastle; A1.
The *Curlew*, *Sophia* and *Jane* passengers were tenants of the Marquis of Breadalbane. After their arrival in Montreal some of the Breadalbane emigrants headed for Cape Breton. They called at P.E.I. on their way and settled there instead.

Sophia of Ayr Greenock	Perthshire: mainly Balquhidder and Kincardine	1818 July	Upper Canada but some settled in PEI.	106 Psgrs

Passenger List: *PRO CO 384/3*.
As for the *Curlew* above.
Vessel Details: Brig, 230 tns., built 1811 Ayr; A1.
See comments for *Curlew*.

Vessel Name Departure Port	Captain Emigrant Geographical Origins	Departure Year	Month	Arrival Month P.E.I. Location (if known)	Passenger Nos.
Jane of Sunderland Greenock	Rogers, James	1818	July (Est.)	Upper Canada but some went to PEI.	? Psgrs

Partial Passenger List: *PRO CO 226/36.*
Vessel Details: Ship, 340 tns., built 1805 Sunderland; E1.
As for the *Curlew* above.

| *Jessie* of Dumfries Dumfries | Williams, James Dumfriesshire, Wigtownshire, Kirkcudbrightshire, and Cumberland | 1819 | April | N/K | ? Psgrs |

DGC 1 June, 1819.
Vessel Details: Brig, 209 tns., built 1814 Dumfries; A1.
The *Jessie* was also bound for the New Brunswick port of Miramichi.

| *Morningfield* of Aberdeen Tobermory | Laing West Highlands & Islands | 1819 | July | N/K | 264 Psgrs |

SRO E504/35/2; *PEIG* 3 Sept. 1819.
Vessel Details: Brig, 141 tns., built 1816 Aberdeen; A1.
The *Morningfield* arrived at Pictou with 64 passengers and at Charlottetown with 200 passengers.

| *Alexander* Greenock | Lyon, R | 1820 | April | N/K | 181 Psgrs |

PEIG 22 May 1820; *QM* 5 June 1820.
Vessel Details: Brig, 169 tns., built 1818 New Carlisle, Quebec; A1.
Eighty five passengers left at P.E.I. and 96 at Quebec.

| *Diana* of Dumfries Dumfries | Martin, John | 1820 | April | N/K | 43 Psgrs |

Jones and Fraser, "Those Elusive Immigrants" (Part 1), p.38; *DWJ*, 15 Feb. 1820.
Vessel Details: Snow, 226 tns., built 1819 Sunderland; A1.
Forty-three passengers left at Charlottetown. The shipping agent, John Walker, stated that he had particulars of land for sale in P.E.I. in his shipping advertisement in the *Dumfries Weekly Journal*.
The *Diana* was due to sail on to Chaleur Bay (New Brunswick).

| *Jessie* of Dumfries Dumfries | Williams, James | 1820 | April | N/K | 179 Psgrs |

DWJ 18 Apr. 1820.

Vessel Name Departure Port	Captain Emigrant Geographical Origins	Departure Year Month	Arrival Month P.E.I. Location (if known)	Passenger Nos.

Vessel Details: See above
The *Jessie*, with 179 passengers, was bound for P.E.I. as well as the New Brunswick ports of Miramichi and Richibucto.

Britannia of Dumfries McDowall		1820	April (Est.)Apr.	90 Psgrs
Dumfries			N/K	

PEIG 22 May 1820; *DWJ* 1 Feb, 18 Apr. 1820.
Vessel Details: Snow, 200 tns., built 1809 Whitehaven; E1.
According to the *P.E.I. Gazette*, 31 passengers landed at P.E.I. The *Dumfries Weekly Journal* stated that the *Britannia* left with 90 passengers. The *Britannia* was also bound for Miramichi (New Brunswick).

Diana of Dumfries	Martin, John	1821	April (Est.)	53 Psgrs
Dumfries			N/K	

PEIG 24 May 1821; *DGC* 27 March 1821.
Vessel Details: See above
53 passengers left at Charlottetown. The *Diana* was due to sail on to Chaleur Bay (New Brunswick).

Thompson's Packet of Dumfries		1821	April (Est.)	80 Psgrs
Dumfries			N/K	

DGC 30 Jan., 10 Apr. 1821.
Vessel Details: Brig, 201 tns., built 1817; A1.
Eighty passengers are known to have left at Pictou but arrivals (if any) at Charlottetown are not known.

Nancy of Dumfries	Kirk, Joseph	1821	May	15 Psgrs
Dumfries			N/K	

DGC 27 March, 1 May 1821.
Vessel Details: Brig, 208 tns., built 1817 Dumfries; A1.

Pallas	Moir	1821	Aug (Est.) Sept.	27 Psgrs
Tobermory	West Highlands & Islands		N/K	

PEIG 22 Sept. 1821; Jones and Fraser, "Those Elusive Immigrants" (Part 1) p. 39.

Commerce of Greenock		1822		? Psgrs
Tobermory	Island of Muck, Inverness-shire		N/K	

MacDonald, 'Early Highland Emigration, PEI', p. 45; Brehaut, 'Early Immigration, PEI.'
Vessel Details: Ship, 425 tns., built 1813 Quebec; A1.
The ship arrived at Plaster Rock, Nova Scotia but many of the *Commerce* passengers moved on to P.E.I..

Vessel Name	Captain		Departure		Arrival	Passenger
Departure Port	Emigrant Geographical Origins		Year	Month	Month	Nos.
					P.E.I. Location (if known)	

Diana of Dumfries Martin, John   1822 April (Est.) May   16 Psgrs
Dumfries   N/K
Jones and Fraser 'Those Elusive Immigrants' (Part 1), p. 39; *DWJ* 21 Feb., 3 Apr. 1822.
Vessel Details: See above
Sixteen passengers left at Charlottetown. The *Diana* was also bound for Chaleur Bay (New Brunswick).

Eliza of Thurso   1823 April (Est.) May   8 Psgrs
Thurso   North East Highlands   N/K
Jones and Fraser, *Ibid.*; SRO E504/7/6
Vessel Details: 204 tns.
The *Eliza* returned to Thurso from the Miramichi, New Brunswick in January 1823.

John Walker   1826   ? Psgrs
                Mainly Skye,   Dundas (Lot 55)
                some Uist
MacDonald, "Early Highland Emigration, PEI," p. 45; Brehaut, "Early Immigration, PEI."

Caroline of Liverpool Rea, James   1828 April   ? Psgrs
Inverness &   West Highlands   N/K
Fort William   & Islands
IJ 29 Feb. 1828; SRO E504 5/1.
According to the *Inverness Journal*, the *Caroline* was due to call at Pictou, P.E.I. and the Miramichi in New Brunswick. Thirty-six passengers are known to have arrived at Pictou, but arrivals at P.E.I. (if any) are unknown. The *Caroline* sailed from Inverness to Fort William via the Caledonian Canal. Fares were £3.10.s. and passengers provided their own food.

Louisa of Aberdeen   1829   170 Psgrs
Stornoway   Skye   Uigg (Lot 50)
Martell, J.S., *Immigration to and Emigration from Nova Scotia 1815–38.* (PANS, 1842) p. 63.
Vessel Details: Barque, 213 tns., built 1816 Aberdeen; E1.
Seventy of the 170 passengers who sailed in the *Louisa* went to P.E.I.. The remainder went to Cape Breton.

Mary Kennedy   1829 April (Est.) May   c. 300 Psgrs
Skye   Mainly Uig in Skye   Uigg (Lot 50).
MacQueen, *Skye Pioneers and the Island.* pp. 72, 93–99; PEIG 2 June 1829.
The *P.E.I. Gazette* reported that 84 immigrants from Skye (who were heads of households) had arrived on a ship, which had called, also at Cape Breton. Given the heads of households arrived with their families, passenger numbers on board the *Mary Kennedy* can be estimated at around 300.

Vessel Name Departure Port	Captain Emigrant Geographical Origins	Departure Year Month	Arrival Month P.E.I. Location (if known)	Passenger Nos.

Vestal
Tobermory — Mainly Skye — 1829 — June (Est.) — Aug. — 301 Psgrs — Many to Lot 50
Jones and Fraser, "Those Elusive Immigrants" (Part 1), p. 41.
Seventy of the Skye emigrants moved on to Cape Breton.

Corsair of Greenock
Greenock — 1830 — 206 Psgrs — Johnston's River (Lot 35)
Warburton, *History of Prince Edward Island*, p.381; *IJ* 6 Aug. 1830; Martell, *Immigration to and Emigration from Nova Scotia*, p. 66.
Vessel Details: Brig, 276 tns, built 1823 New Brunswick, AE1.
Rev. John MacDonald led this group of Roman Catholics, who included some from Ireland. Most settled near Johnston's River in P.E.I. but around 40 are known to have disembarked from this ship at Canso, Cape Breton.

Lord Mulgrave — Cordingly
of Whitby — 1830 — N/K — ? Psgrs
MacDonald, "Early Highland Emigration, PEI," p. 46.
Vessel Details: Ship, 414 tns., built 1807 Whitby; E1.

Mary Kennedy
Tobermory — Mainly Skye — 1831 — N/K — 80 Psgrs
Brehaut, "Early Immigration, PEI," p. 46; MacQueen, *Skye Pioneers*. p. 93.

Staffa
Greenock — West Highlands & Islands — 1831 — April (Est.) May — N/K — 65 Psgrs
Jones and Fraser, 'Those Elusive Immigrants' (Part 2), p. 34.
Vessel Details: Brig, 268 tns., built 1830 PEI; A1.
Mr and Mrs Angus MacDonald and 63 in steerage. The *Staffa* landed at Three Rivers.

Mary Ann
Tobermory — West Highlands & Islands — 1831 — Aug (Est.) Sept. — N/K — ? Psgrs
Jones and Fraser, *Ibid.*
The *Mary Ann* landed some passengers at Point Prim.

Staffa
Greenock — West Highlands & Islands — 1831 — Aug (Est.) Sept. — N/K — 156 Psgrs
Jones and Fraser, *Ibid.*

Vessel Name Departure Port	Captain Emigrant Geographical Origins	Departure Year	Month	Arrival Month P.E.I. Location (if known)	Passenger Nos.

Vessel Details: See above.
Colin MacDonald and 155 in steerage. The *Staffa* landed at Three Rivers.

| *Phoenix*
Greenock | | 1832 | April (Est.) | N/K | c. 150
Psgrs |

Jones and Fraser, *Ibid.*, p. 35.
Twelve families (30 to 40 people) left at Three Rivers. Another 30 to 40 families landed at Pictou.
All were reported to be in good health.

| *Amity*
Tobermory | West Highlands
& Islands | 1833 | July (Est.) | Aug.
N/K | 258 Psgrs |

Brehaut, "Early Immigration, PEI," Martell, *Immigration to and Emigration from Nova Scotia.* p. 77.
258 passengers arrived at Ship Harbour, Cape Breton. An unknown number later moved on to
P.E.I..

| *Pekin* of Liverpool
Stornoway | Skye | 1839 | July (Est.) | Aug.
Some to Lot 67 | 266 Psgrs |

Jones and Fraser, "Those Elusive Immigrants" (Part 3), p. 33.
Vessel Details: Brig, 288 tns., built 1833 Quebec; AE1.

| *Nith*
Uig & Tobermory | Mainly Skye | 1840 | July (Est.) | Sept.
Many to Belfast area | 550 Psgrs |

Jones and Fraser, *Ibid.*; *IC* 12 Aug. 1840.
Some 400 passengers boarded at Uig and 150 at Tobermory. Ninety-seven passengers disembarked
at Sydney, while 315 left at Charlottetown.

| *Rother*
Tobermory | Skye | 1840 | July (Est.) | Sept.
Many to Belfast area | 229 Psgrs |

Jones and Fraser, *Ibid.* p. 34.
Vessel Details: Schooner, 270 tns., built 1835 Sunderland; A1.

| *Heroine* of Aberdeen
Stornoway | Skye | 1840 | Aug (Est.) | Sept.
Many to Belfast area | 281 Psgrs |

Jones and Fraser, *Ibid.*
Vessel Details: Ship, 387 tns., built Dundee 1831; AE1.

| *Ocean* of Liverpool
Portree, Skye | McKenzie, George
Skye | 1841 | June (Est.) | July
Most to Belfast area | 335 Psgrs |

Ibid., p. 35.

Vessel Name Departure Port	Captain Emigrant Geographical Origins	Departure Year Month	Arrival Month P.E.I. Location (if known)	Passenger Nos.
Washington of Liverpool Uig, Skye	McLay Skye	1841 June (Est.)	Aug. Most to Belfast area	551 Psgrs

Ibid. MacLeod, Harold S., *The MacLeods of Prince Edward Island.* (Montague, PEI, 1986) p.xv.
The passengers came from Kilmuir, Snizort and other parishes on the east side of Skye.

Cleostratus Glasgow	Levens	1842 June (Est.)	N/K	? Psgrs

AH 30 Apr. 1842; *GH* 18 Apr. 1842.
Sixty-four passengers arrived at Pictou in August. The *Aberdeen Herald* stated that the *Cleostratus* would be landing passengers at P.E.I..

Symmetry Thurso	North East Highlands	1843 April	N/K	128 Psgrs

PP1844(181)xxxv.
The *Symmetry* sailed to Quebec with 128 passengers. The Quebec arrivals were described as being in good circumstances. Around 18 emigrants had disembarked at P.E.I. and Pictou.

Ann Elizabeth Psgrs Leith		1846 April (Est.)	June N/K	?

Fraser, Douglas, "More Elusive Immigrants" (Part 4), p. 39.

Lord Sidmouth Glasgow		1846 Aug (Est.)	Oct. N/K	? Psgrs

Ibid., p. 40.

Ellen of Liverpool Loch Laxford	McLachlan, Dugald Sutherland	1848 May	Lot 21	154 Psgrs

Passenger List: McLaren, George, *The Pictou Book.* (1954) pp. 108–110.
Morse, Susan Longley, "Immigration to Nova Scotia 1839–51" (Dalhousie, N.S., unpublished M.A. 1946) pp. 98–9.
Vessel Details: Barque, 397 tns., built 1834 New Brunswick; AE1.
An unknown number of the 154 emigrants who arrived at Pictou later settled in P.E.I. .A customs official at Pictou commented that the Captain "acted indeed onto one and all of them, the passengers, more like the head of a family than a shipmaster. No praise that they can bestow on him can be too great." The ship had been chartered by the Duke of Sutherland. A head tax was levied on all passengers. A dispute broke out because the families who went to P.E.I. had to pay the head tax twice.

Lulan of Pictou   McKenzie, George   1848   Aug   167 Psgrs
Glasgow   South Uist   Some to Lot 54
Passenger List: McLaren, *Ibid.*, pp. 114–18.
Morse, *Ibid.*
Vessel Details: Barque, 473 tns., built 1848 Pictou, N.S.; A1.
Seventy-two of the 167 emigrants who travelled on the *Lulan* eventually moved to P.E.I. The emigrants were assisted by their landlord, Col. John Gordon. Unknown to the emigrants, they were initially put on a ship bound for Boston, but the error was discovered in time. After leaving their ship, they had to wait a long time in the Clyde for a ship which would take them to Pictou. They arrived in Pictou on the *Lulan* suffering from disease and extreme poverty. The ships that took them on to P.E.I. and Cape Breton were hired at public expense. In all, there were 9 cabin and 158 steerage passengers who included 30 men with families who intended to work in the Albion Coal Mines near Pictou. The captain, George McKenzie was a prominent Pictou shipbuilder who later moved his yards to New Glasgow. He became known as the "father of shipbuilding" having a reputation for building superior ships which he usually sailed himself.

NOTES

CHAPTER 1 — PUSH, PULL AND OPPORTUNITY

1 Prince Edward Island Genealogical Society, From Scotland to Prince Edward Island: *Scottish emigrants to Prince Edward Island from death and obituary notices in Prince Edward Island 1835–1910* (n.d.), Cem. Transc., p. 14. Hereafter this source is referred to as PEI Gen. Soc., Survey.

2 Through his writings, Selkirk promoted emigration generally and, in all, he sponsored three major colonisation schemes, the most successful being his settlement at Belfast.

3 Clark, Andrew, Hill, *Three centuries and the Island: A historical geography of settlement and agriculture in Prince Edward Island, Canada.* (Toronto: University of Toronto Press, 1959) pp. 55–7.

4 Clark, *Ibid,* p. 90. Data on place of origin as opposed to place of birth was not reliably gathered until 1881.

5 Population figures for Kings County from Clark, *Ibid,* p. 125. Also see *Prince Edward Island Census Abstract, 1848.*

6 PEI Gen. Soc. *Survey* refers either to PEI lot numbers or PEI place names. Where place names are given, their corresponding lot number locations have been obtained from Rayburn, Alan, *Geographical Names of Prince Edward Island; Toponymy Study.* (Ottawa: Department of Energy, Mines and Resources, 1973).

7 In the initial stages of settlement, resources would have been scarce and opportunities to commemorate the dead extremely limited. However, the records show that a great many descendants of the original pioneers erected tombstones at a later stage on behalf of their earlier relatives.

8 Only one partial passenger list and ten full lists survive for crossings in 1771, 1774, 1775, 1790, 1806 and 1808.

9 From as early as 1790, Prince Edward Island newspapers sometimes reported emigrant ship arrivals and occasionally emigrant departures were reported by Scottish newspapers.

10 Davis, Ralph, *The Industrial Revolution and British Overseas Trade.* (Leicester: Leicester University Press, 1979) pp. 48–49. Duties increased from 25s. per load in 1804 to 54s.6d. per load in 1811. Between 1814 and 1843 Baltic timber was sometimes shipped to North America and then back to Britain, as the saving of duty more than compensated for the double freight.

11 Unlike British North America's other major resource commodities (fish, fur and grain), timber was extremely bulky and generated a huge increase in the volume of shipping.

12 The most direct and probably the most influential source of encouragement to potential emigrants was the private correspondence sent by established settlers to their families and friends back home in Scotland. Private letters from trusted loved ones would have carried far more weight than official government periodicals and guides. Regrettably few personal letters survive, since they were normally not intended for publication.

13 Kelp is burnt scaweed used in the manufacture of soap and glass; it was very profitable during the Napoleonic Wars when imports of foreign material were blocked. It was produced on the west coast of Scotland and in the Western Isles. It was loaded onto ships and exported, and employed a large amount of labour. Scottish kelp production declined after the wars ended in 1815. It was virtually wiped out by the 1820s as cheap imports of equivalent material broke into its former market.

14 Johnston, H. J. M., *British emigration policy 1815–1830: Shovelling out paupers.* (Oxford: Clarendon Press, 1972) pp. 110–128; Harper, Marjory, *Emigration from North-East Scotland* Vol. 1, *Willing Exiles.* (Aberdeen: Aberdeen University Press 1988) pp. 18–20,126–8.

15 Douglas, Thomas, fifth Earl of Selkirk, *Observations on the present state of the Highlands of Scotland with a view of the causes and probable consequences of emigration.* (Edinburgh, 1806) pp. 116–24.

16 Landlords varied enormously in their generosity and willingness to fund emigration costs; see for example Mackenzie, John Munro, *Diary for 1851 of John Munro Mackenzie Chamberlain of the Lews.* (Stornoway, Isle of Lewis: Acair, 1994) and Devine, T. M., *The Great Highland Famine, Hunger, Emigration and the Scottish Highlands in the Nineteenth Century.* (Edinburgh: John Donald, 1988) pp. 323–6.

17 PEI immigrant totals from 1848 to 1851 were: from Ireland 1,214, from Scotland 1,055 and from England 347 (SRO GD 51/15/58).

18 Comparative studies of emigration across Europe show that emigration surges were determined more by the prospect of prosperity in another country than by adverse conditions at home. The peaks and troughs in nineteenth century emigration levels were fairly consistent across Europe, even though the countries from which people were emigrating experienced very different economic and social conditions. Baines, Dudley, *Emigration from Europe 1815–1930.* (Basingstoke: Macmillan, 1991) pp. 7–15,24–25,31–38.

CHAPTER II — THE FIRST ARRIVALS FROM SCOTLAND

1 PEI Gen. Soc., *Survey, Cem. Transc,* p.3.

2 When the Mi'kmaq Indians, who numbered around 2,000, declared war on Britain in 1749 in retaliation for the creation of a British military presence and settlement at Halifax, they were faced with a policy of extermination. With the defeat of the French at Louisbourg in 1758, the Mi'kmaq were forced to surrender to British control losing much of their land in Nova Scotia, Cape Breton and

the Island of Saint John to Loyalist settlers who came from the southern colonies from 1784.

3 The proprietors were to get land, upon payment of a quit rent (a feudal term meaning a payment made by tenants to their laird to excuse them from the customary manor services) assessed at rates ranging from two shillings to six shillings per 100 acres, and had to agree to settle their lands within ten years, at the rate of 100 people per township. It was also agreed that the quit rent revenues would be used to finance the Island's government, which was established on the Island some two years later in 1769. The condition that the new government's expenses would be paid from the proceeds of quit rents was not honoured by the proprietors in spite of repeated attempts to force them to pay. Interestingly, quit rent was only fully abolished in Britain in 1922. Bolger, F. W. P. (ed.) *Canada's Smallest Province: A History of Prince Edward Island.* (Halifax: Nimbus, 1991) pp. 42–3.

4 Clark, *Three Centuries and the Island.* pp. 48–52; Bolger, *Ibid, pp.* 38–42.

5 The leasehold system was only completely abolished in 1873 when Prince Edward Island entered the Canadian Confederation. Bumsted, J. M., *Land Settlement and Politics in Eighteenth Century Prince Edward Island.* (Kingston: McGill Queens, 1987) pp. 196–200; Clark, *Ibid* 91–95.

6 PAPEI 3846: Bumsted, 'The Scottish Catholic Church and Prince Edward Island 1770–1810' pp. 18–19; Roberston, Ian, Ross 'Highlanders, Irishmen and the Land Question in Nineteenth Century Prince Edward Island' in J. M. Bumsted (ed.), *Interpreting Canada's Past; Vol. 1.* (Toronto: Oxford University Press, 1986) pp. 359–73. Clark, *Ibid,* p. 50.

7 Even by as late as 1841, less than a quarter of the land in over half of the townships was freehold.

8 Argyll emigrants had established themselves in the southern colonies thirty years before the proprietor-led expedition of the early 1770's to Prince Edward Island. While some went to New York, the great majority were family groups who settled in North Carolina. They mainly originated from the islands of Islay, Jura and Gigha and from these mainland parishes: Appin, Lismore, Glenorchy and Campbeltown, North and South Knapdale and Inishail. Meyer, D. Vane, *The Highland Scots of North Carolina.* (Durham: University of Carolina Press, 1961) pp. 84,86; Adams, Ian and Somerville, Meredyth, *Cargoes of Despair and Hope: Scottish emigration to North America 1603–1803* (Edinburgh : John Donald, 1993) pp. 87,89, 90, 218; Cameron, Viola Root, *Emigrants from Scotland to America 1774–1775.* (Baltimore: Genealogical Publishing Co., 1965) pp. 88–90.

9 James Montgomery got lot 7 in the lottery and acquired lots 30, 34, 36 and 51 by 1770. Bumsted, *Land Settlement and Politics.* p. 51

10 Bumsted, *Ibid, p.* 53. David Lawson was even thought to have been too successful in attracting Perthshire emigrants to Stanhope.

11 After serving a four year indenture, those who remained, would have been entitled to 200 to 500 acres of wilderness land per man on easy terms.

12 Bumsted, J. M., *The People's Clearance: Highland emigration to British North America 1770 –1815.* (Edinburgh: Edinburgh University Press, 1982) pp. 56–57; MacEwan, Andrew, B. W., 'The Falmouth Passengers', *The Island Magazine,*

vol.10 (1981) pp. 12–19; PEI Gen. Soc. *Survey* shows regular arrivals at Stanhope from 1800 to 1808. The *Clarendon* arrived at Charlottetown in 1808 with mainly Perthshire emigrants; see PRO CO 226/23 pp. 199–208.

13 *SM,* vol. XXXIII (1771) p. 379.

14 Peter Stewart leased a part of lot 34 from Sir James Montgomery. Although he initially had high hopes of becoming a successful farmer, he died severely in debt to Montgomery. Adams and Somerville, *Cargoes of Despair.* p 59.

15 The Malpeque Bay area acquired some Loyalist settlers in 1784–85, although numbers and location are unknown; Clark, *Three Centuries and the Island.* pp. 57–58. Bumsted, *Land Settlement and Politics.* pp. 50–51; Malpeque Historical Society, *Malpeque and Its People 1700–1982* (Malpeque, 1982) pp. 25, 52–57. For a description of the vessel crossings see Lawson, Rev. James, "Early Scottish Settlements on Prince Edward Island: The Princetown Pioneers, 1769–1771," *SG,* vol. xli (1994) pp. 112–30 and "Passengers on the *Alexander,*" *SG,* vol. xxxix (1992) pp. 127–43; The *Edinburgh* also carried passengers whose fares had been paid by a Hugh Montgomery, suggesting that they may have been destined for the Montgomery settlement at Stanhope; a partial passenger list survives for the *Edinburgh* - see SRO SC 54/2/106. In 1771, *The Scots Magazine* reported that 100 settlers had been brought out to the Island in 1770 (*SM,* vol. xxx p. 379).

16 Roman Catholics had to wait until 1832 before they could vote.

17 Tacksmen were an elite class in the Scottish feudal system who acted as factors or farm managers under a laird. They usually sublet much of their own land to sub-tenants who did most of the work on the great Highland estates. With the introduction of improved farming methods in the 1770s the tacksmen's role became increasingly obsolete and many reacted to the sweeping changes by promoting emigration within their local population and were highly influential in encouraging large numbers to emigrate.

18 For example John Morrow, Sarah MacInnes and Donald Beaton were 1772 arrivals at lot 47: PEI Gen. Soc., *Survey,* pp. 3,27,46.

19 Bumsted, *Land Settlement and Politics.* pp. 57–61; Bumsted, "The Scottish Catholic Church," pp. 18–19.

20 HCA FAM/INV/25/1: Photocopy of letter from John MacDonald of Glenaladale to his cousin Alexander MacDonald in Jamaica, 7 March 1772; MacKay, Ian, R., "Glenaladale's Settlement in Prince Edward Island," *Scottish Gaelic Studies,* vol. x (1965) pp. 17–20.

21 SCA, Blairs Letters 3/269/3.

22 Passenger lists for the *Jane* and *Lucy* (1790) are to be found in Appendix i.

23 *Prince Edward Island Royal Gazette,* 29 July, 1791.

24 *Ibid,* 9 Sept. 1791.

25 *Ibid.*

26 Letter to Colin MacDonald, 22 Oct. 1791: NLS Adv. MS.73.2.13 f. 27.

27 *PEI Royal Gazette,* 30 May 1794;

28 Nine hundred of the 1,300 population in 1775 had arrived during the previous 5 years and Scottish Catholics made up the majority.   Bumsted, *Land Settlement and Politics.* p. 168; Bumsted, "The Scottish Catholic Church" pp. 26–27;

29 MacNutt, W. S., *The Atlantic Provinces; the emergence of Colonial Society*

1712–1857. (London: McClelland and Stewart, 1965) pp. 117–18; Campbell, D.F. and R.A. MacLean, *Beyond the Atlantic Roar: A Study of the Nova Scotia Scots.* (Toronto: McClelland and Stewart, 1974) pp. 210–13; Moir, John S., *The Church in the British Era, from the British Conquest to Confederation.* (Toronto: McGraw-Hill Ryerson, 1972) pp. 135–37.

30 The officers included; Col. Simon Fraser, Lt. Col. James Abercrombie, Lt. Col. John Campbell and Capt. John MacDonnell.

31 *The Scottish Catholics in Prince Edward Island 1772–1922.* Memorial Volume (Summerside: Journal Publishing Co., 1922) pp. 47–54. According to the 1848 Census, Roman Catholic predominance measured over 50 % in 38, 41, 43, 47, 53 and 55; over 75 % in lot 54 and over 90 % in lots 42, 45 and 46.

32 Many were artisans and labourers and may not have had farming skills: *PRO T47/12.*

33 PAPEI Acc 2779/1. Samuel Smith was agent to the Crown for the Island.

34 White, Patrick Cecil Telford, (ed.) *Lord Selkirk's Diary 1803–04; A journal of his travels through British North America and the Northeastern United States.* (Toronto: The Champlain Society, 1958) p. 49.

35 Sinclair, Sir John, *First Statistical Account of Scotland.* 21 vols. (Edinburgh, 1791–99) vol. iv, pp. 69, 290–91.

CHAPTER III — THE SELKIRK SETTLERS OF 1803

1 Warburton, A. B., *A History of Prince Edward Island* (St. John, N.B., 1923) p. 269.

2 Although the Macdonald's are strongly associated with their Scottish estates, the first title was established in the Irish peerage. The title dates back to 1776, when Sir Alexander Macdonald, 9th baronet was created an Irish peer, becoming Baron Macdonald of Slate in County Antrim. Following his death in 1795, he was succeeded by his eldest son Alexander Wentworth Macdonald, 2nd Baron. Godfrey Macdonald Bosville inherited the title in 1824 as 3rd Lord. Godfrey William Wentworth Macdonald acquired the title as 4th Lord in 1832 and held the title until his death in 1863.

3 MacAuley lived on the Island until his death in 1827. MacAuley was elected to the House of Assembly in 1806 and became speaker of the House in 1818. *Dictionary of Canadian Biography,* vol. VI, 412–15.

4 *SRO GD* 221/4433/1 (paper watermarked 1802).

5 PAPEI 2704/4.

6 There is some dispute about the origin of the name Belfast. Selkirk's reference to Belfast in his diary of 1803 was to "the settlement at the old French village called Belfast"—hence the theory developed that it was a French name. I have followed the explanation given in Rayburn, Alan, *Geographical Names of Prince Edward Island; Toponymy Study* (Ottawa: Department of Energy, Mines and Resources, 1973). This credits the naming of Belfast to Captain James Smith of HMS *Mermaid* who named the settlement after Belfast, Ireland c. 1770. This naming was reported in *The Gentlemen's Magazine,* London, March 1771. In checking the list of people who were granted lots as a result of the 1767 lottery I have found that lot 57 was owned jointly by Samuel Smith merchant (leader of the 1775 expedi-

tion), and James Smith, Captain in the Navy. (Bolger, *Canada's Smallest Province*, pp. 39–41).

7 Data from death notices and tombstones reveals that at least two of the Morayshire families stayed on the Island. See Chapter 2 for further details of the Morayshire expedition.

8 The Passenger Act of 1803 introduced minimum space and food requirements for passengers in ocean-going vessels. Passenger numbers were restricted to one passenger for every two tons of the vessel. Minimum daily food provisions for each passenger were: 1/2 lb. meat; 1 and 1/2 lbs. bread, biscuit or oatmeal; 1/2 pint molasses; 1 gallon water. The Act was largely unenforceable and thus frequently ignored.

9 Skye settlers went to North Carolina in several spurts from 1771 to 1775; large numbers originated from Duirinish and Bracadale. See *SM*, vol. XXXIII (1771) p. 501; Graham, Ian Charles Cargill, *Colonists from Scotland: Emigration to North America 1707–83* (New York: Cornell University Press, 1956) p. 76; Meyer, *Highland Scots*, p. 86; Adams and Somerville, *Cargoes of Despair*, p. 96; Sinclair, *First Statistical Account*, vol. xx, p. 155,160–61. *Colonial Records of North Carolina*, vol. viii (1771) pp. 620–21.

10 Douglas, Thomas, fifth Earl of Selkirk, *Observations on the Present State of the Highlands of Scotland, with a view of the causes and probable consequences of emigration,* (Edinburgh, 1806) p. 168.

11 The apparent ease with which Prince Edward Island became a magnet for Skye settlers at this time suggests that there may have been earlier, pre-1803 Skye footholds on the Island. We have to look to the many Bracadale and Duirinish emigrants, some of whom included "people of property," who had previously settled in North Carolina in the early 1770s. Possibly some of these people, or their descendants, may have been relocated to the Island as Loyalists in the late 1780s, following the end of the American War.

12 Details of vessel crossings from Telford, Thomas, *A Survey and Report of the Coasts and Central Highlands of Scotland* (London, 1803), Prince Edward Island customs records (*PAPEI RG9*) and from White, *Lord Selkirk's Diary* , pp. 4, 6, 35. The departure of the *Oughton* was reported in the *Glasgow Herald* 24 June, 1803.

13 These ships appear in the 1803 *Lloyds Shipping Register*. A ship's ranking was determined by criteria relating to overall construction, age, state of repairs, type and quality of materials used and the place where the ship was built. Ships designated as "A" are "of the first class" and newly built; as "E" are "second description of the first class," indicating that they have no defects but are over a prescribed age limit. The number "1" following the letter designates materials used in building the ships were "of the first quality," while "2" designates that the materials used were "of the second quality."

14 *Glasgow Courier* , 9 April, 1803. Information in Thomas Telford's survey of 1803 confirms that the *Polly* was due to go on to New Brunswick, probably to collect a timber cargo.

15 SRO CS 96/1238: McKnight and McIlwraith, Haberdashers, Ayr (1802–03); SRO CS 96/1534 and 1535: John MacDonald and Co. Merchants, Montreal (1799–1804).

16 SRO CS 96/1238: Letters to John MacDonald, 28 June and 12 Aug. 1803.

17 *Ibid:* Letter to Captain Baird of ship *Oughton* 12 Aug. 1803.

18 The *Polly* arrived on 7th August, the *Dykes* on the 9th August and the *Oughton* on 27th August.

19 The petition begins: "We the undersigned beg leave to express our gratitude and respect to the Reverend Doctor Angus MacAuley for his unremitted attention in keeping alive true Christian devotion and piety for seven years among us. The greatest part being unacquainted with the English tongue would be totally deprived of clerical instruction were it not for his knowledge of the Gaelic language." The list of names appears in PAPEI 2704/4 and in MacQueen, Malcolm A., *Hebridean Pioneers,* (Winnipeg, 1957) pp. 73–4.

20 The job had gone to a businessman, James Williams, who arrived after MacAuley on the *Oughton.*

21 *Dictionary of Canadian Biography,* Vol. VI pp. 413–15; Martin, Chester, *Lord Selkirk's Work in Canada* , Oxford Historical and Literary Studies, vol. 7 (Oxford, 1916) p. 178–79.

22 "Each of them [settlements] was inhabited by persons nearly related, who was always at hand to come to each others' assistance and in some instances carried on all their work in common,": Douglas, *Observations on the Present State of the Highlands,* p. 176. White, *Lord Selkirk's Diary,* p. 35. Also see Macqueen, Malcolm, *Skye Pioneers and the Island* (Winnipeg: Stovel Co., 1929) pp. 13–14.

23 White, *Ibid,* pp. 7, 35.

24 *Dictionary of Canadian Biography,* Vol. VI, pp. 414–15.

25 White, *Lord Selkirk's Diary,* pp. 35, 37.

26 White, *Ibid.* pp. 32–33; Donald MacRae, died 1868; Duncan MacRae, died 1847; Duncan MacRae, died 1872; Duncan MacRae, died 1874; Finlay MacRae, died 1862; Malcolm MacRae, died 1847. See PEI Gen. Soc., *Survey:* pp. 29, 31, 32, 42, 43.

27 Douglas, *Observations on the Present State of the Highlands,* pp. 174–75.

28 *Ibid,* p. 175.

29 *Ibid,* p. 178.

30 Selkirk's holdings of 143,000 acres comprised lots 10 (20,000 ac.), 31 (20,000 ac.), 57 (20,000 ac.), 58 (20,000 ac.) , 60 (20,000 ac.) and 62 (20,000 ac.); one-half of lot 12 (10,000 ac.), one-third of lot 53 (6,686 ac.) and one-third of lot 59 (6,686 ac.). Lots 57, 58, 60 and 62 which fall within Queens County were the Belfast townships. Martin, *Lord Selkirk's Work,* p. 177.

31 By 1848, lots 60 and 62 could claim Presbyterian affiliations for more than ninety per cent of their populations, and lots 57 and 58 for over seventy five per cent. *Prince Edward Island Census Abstracts,* 1848.

32 Data obtained from tombstone inscriptions and death notices reveals that most South Uist and Barra emigrants, who were mainly Roman Catholic, settled in Kings County, with small clusters identifiable at lots 41 and 55.

33 Macqueen, *Skye Pioneers,* p. 36.

34 John McGregor, the Island's High Sheriff, quoted in Warburton, *Prince Edward Island,* p. 285.

CHAPTER IV — THE COMING OF THE TIMBER TRADE

1   Lawson, John, *Letters on Prince Edward Island by John Lawson, Esq., barrister at law and Judge Advocate* (Charlottetown, 1851), Letter X, p. 37: *SRO GD 51/15/58*

2   *Ibid.* James' father may be Duncan McCallum of Argyll, who emigrated in 1771 and died 1844, aged 89. At the time of his death he resided in lot 33, the township in which Brackley Point is located. PEI Gen. Soc. *Survey, Cem. Transc.*, p. 14.

3   For example, in 1791, the *Jean* of London carried timber from Pictou, Nova Scotia to Fort William for Allan Cameron, a local merchant: SRO E504/12/3.

4   Greenhill, Basil and Anne Giffard, *Westcountrymen in Prince Edward's Isle* (Toronto: University of Toronto Press, 1967) pp. 28,47.

5   It was claimed that the Island imported annually British manufactured goods valued at between £40,000 to £45,000. Evidence of John Hill, a London merchant to the *The Select Committee on Foreign Trade*, March, 1821, published in *Prince Edward Island Gazette*, 8 Sept., 1821.

6   Hon. Mr. Haviland, in *Prince Edward Island Royal Gazette*, 6 Dec. 1825.

7   *Inverness Journal*, 22 March 1811.

8   SRO CS 96/4475: Letter dated 7 April 1810 from John MacKenzie, shipowner and merchant from Stornoway to Mr. R. Thornton of Liverpool..

9   A total of six vessels left from Oban, six from Tobermory, two from Stornoway, one from Fort William and one from Thurso.

10 Journal concerning emigration from Blair Atholl to Prince Edward Island, 1808: *NLS MS 11976 ff. 3–4.*

11 Bumsted, *People's Clearance*, pp. 202–3.

12 *PAPEI MSS, 2702; PAPEI RG9 #1; SRO E504/25/3,35/1*; PRO CO 226/23; *Greenock Advertiser*, 11 June 1806.

13 The *Clarendon* list is in PRO CO 226/23; the remainder are to be found in *PAPEI MSS 2702*

14 It was generally accepted throughout Scotland that the Act would provide a temporary deterrent to emigration and allow time for the Highland improvement schemes, being recommended at the time by Thomas Telford, to take effect. Macdonagh, Oliver, *A pattern of government growth 1800–1860; the Passenger Acts and their enforcement* (London: MacGibbon and Kee, 1961); also see Bumsted, *The People's Clearance*, pp. 142–5.

15 Government attempts to protect the emigrant from over-zealous shipowners and agents made little practical difference. In the end emigrant travel was transformed for the better, not by legislation, but through the arrival in the 1850s of specialist steam ships. It was then that technology combined with capital investment and competition to bring affordable, consumer-friendly services to the masses.

16 *Inverness Journal*, 28 Dec. 1810, 1 Feb. 1811.

17 Shippers were criticised for charging up to £10 for steerage fares. The legislation required that a vessel should carry one person (adult or child) for every two tons burthen and specified minimum amounts per day of meat and of bread, biscuit or oatmeal and of molasses and water. Shippers argued that, because the regulations did not distinguish between adults and children, the food and space

requirements of the Act usually meant that they carried excessive stocks of food and used space inefficiently.

18 Comments in a Journal, July, 1808 of Gilbert second Earl of Minto, recorded during a visit to Blair Atholl on extensive current emigration from the district to Prince Edward Island and its deliberate stimulation by emigration agents: *NLS MS 11976 ff. 3–4.*

19 Greenhill and Giffard, *Westcountrymen, PEI,* pp. 46–51. The Three Rivers area included parts of lots 51, 52 and 53.

20 Wynn, Graeme, *Timber Colony: an historical geography of early nineteenth century New Brunswick* (Toronto: University of Toronto Press, 1981) pp. 84–86,110–111,113–137.

21 White, *Lord Selkirk's Diary,* p. 44.

22 Clark, *Three Centuries and the Island,* pp. 72, 117, 119.

23 On taking over the business in 1833, his son Hugh transferred its headquarters to Georgetown. *The Scottish Catholics in Prince Edward Island,* pp. 47–54.

24 *SRO E504/35/1.*

25 *Prince Edward Island Register,* 18 March 1825.

26 *NLS MS 11976 ff. 3–4.*

27 PEI Gen. Soc. *Survey* shows that most arrivals from Perthshire to lot 52, with surviving death records giving date of arrival, came to the Island between 1809 and 1818.

28 For example, even ships leaving from east coast ports, such as Aberdeen or Leith, would often call at Tobermory in Mull to collect emigrants on their way to North America to collect timber.

29 Lawson, *Letters on PEI,* Letter X, p. 43.

30 PEI Gen. Soc. *Survey* shows substantial numbers from Sutherland in lots 20 and 21, who in the majority of cases (where detailed origins are given) came from Durness.

31 PEI Gen. Soc. *Survey.* Nicholson, John et al., *Middle River, Past and Present history of a Cape Breton community 1806–1985* (Cape Breton, 1985) pp. 1, 245–47.

32 From the 1790s many Roman Catholics from west Inverness-shire settled in Cape Breton and, after the Napoleonic Wars, Upper Canada also won favour.

33 Beaton Point was established by a group who included Donald Beaton from Lochaber. They were joined by some of the Selkirk settlers in 1803–1804, one of whom was also a Beaton.

34 The emigrants originated mainly from Callander and Killin. The government's decision, in 1815, to subsidise emigration costs with public funds had an air of panic. This had been prompted by the American invasion of 1812 which had demonstrated the vulnerability of the southern border and led to the settlement of loyal civilians in key areas.

35 They had sailed on the *Sophia* and *Curlew* (passenger lists in PRO CO 384/3).

36 Their petition is to be found in: *PRO CO 226/36* p. 19; Also see *Scottish Catholics in Prince Edward Island,* pp. 58–59 and Cowan, Helen, *British Emigration to British North America; the first hundred years* (Toronto: University of Toronto Press, 1961) pp. 44–45.

37 Some included emigrants from the nearby Island of Raasay.

38 Emigration peaked during periods of economic depression. The collapse of the kelp industry would have been a critical factor in the high numbers. In 1841, over 80 % of the people in Argyle Shore (lot 30) and nearly 70% in the adjoining township of New Argyle (lot 65) were Presbyterian. PRO 226/63 p. 194: *Census of the Population and Statistical Return of Prince Edward Island, taken in the year 1841.*

39 From 1816, the Clyde ceased to have a near monopoly on transatlantic trade and the ports of Aberdeen, Dundee and Dumfries started to offer regular Atlantic crossings. However, unlike these other ports which established links with both Maritime and St. Lawrence ports, Dumfries' links were initially mainly with the Maritimes.

Chapter v — Emigrants from Dumfriesshire

1 *A Series of Letters descriptive of Prince Edward Island, in the Gulf of St. Lawrence addressed to the Rev. John Wightman, minister of Kirkmahoe, Dumfriesshire.* An extract from one of the nine letters taken from Harvey, Daniel Cobb (ed.), *Journeys to the Island of Saint John or Prince Edward Island 1775–1832* (Toronto: MacMillan Co. of Canada, 1955) pp. 142–43.

2 Unlike most writers of emigrant guides, Johnstone was not an academic. His knowledge of agriculture and keen critical powers of observation were his strengths and probably made his letters of greater practical benefit to emigrants than most publications of this type.

3 For example see the *Dumfries and Galloway Courier,* 12 March 1822.

4 Cowan, *British Emigration,* p. 52. Not all of these people necessarily settled in British America. Some may have been en-route to the United States. Ports in the Maritimes became well-trodden gateways to the United States, since by using them, British settlers could avoid American immigration taxes.

5 Bolger, *Canada's Smallest Province,* p. 338.

6 *Prince Edward Island Register,* 17 June, 15 Nov. 1825.

7 Appendix to Walter Johnstone's "Letters and Travels" in Harvey, *Journeys to the Island,* pp. 129–32.

8 *Lovelly Nelly* passenger lists in PRO T47/12 (Appendix i).

9 Table 5 lists known emigrant ship crossings. Given the haphazard nature of the available documentary sources, it is highly likely that many emigrant ship crossings went unrecorded.

10 In 1820, the *Diana, Jessie* and *Britannia* between them carried at least 300 passengers to the Island and in 1821 the *Diana, Thompson's Packet* and *Nancy* took about 150.

11 *Parliamentary Papers,* Emigration returns for British North America, 1830–1840.

12 By 1784, there were estimated to be about 500 to 600 Loyalists on the Island. Although the documentary evidence is far from clear, it is thought that most Loyalist settlers took up residence within the Isthmus between Malpeque and Bedeque Bay (lots 16,17,19, 25 and 26). Bolger, *Canada's Smallest Province,* p. 60.

13 SRO GD 51/15/50, pp. 15–6.

14 PEI Gen. Soc. *Survey,* p. 47.

15 However, the name, New Annan, was not apparently coined until the 1830s.

16 Cameron, *Emigrants from Scotland*, pp. 29, 35–40, 73–75.

17 See the passenger lists for the 1774 and 1775 *Lovelly Nelly* crossings (Appendix i). Also see Sinclair, *First Statistical Account*, vol. v, pp. 8, 202, 290–91.

18 Scots were the first to colonise the Miramichi area, arriving in 1785. The Glasgow merchants, Pollock, Gilmour and Company opened up the Miramichi branch of their company in 1812 and soon became the dominant employer on the river's northern bank. In 1824 the Miramichi overtook Saint John as New Brunswick's main timber-exporting port, shipping nearly 142,000 tons of squared timber.

19 For example see the 1851 *Census Returns* for Alnwick, Newcastle, Glenelg, Chatham, North Esk and Nelson parishes in Northumberland County (PANB, 1994).

20 Ganong, W. F., "Monograph *of origins of settlements in the province of New Brunswick*" in Transactions of the Royal Society of Canada, second series (10) ,sections 1–2 (1904) p. 163.

21 Glasgow Colonial Society, *First Annual Report of the Glasgow Colonial Society for promoting the religious interests of Scottish settlers in British North America* (Glasgow, 1826).

22 Ganong, *Ibid,* p. 133.

23 Where Scottish county origins were recorded in the 1861 *Census Returns* for Weldford (Kent County), they mainly show Dumfriesshire. There were much smaller numbers who were recorded as having originated from the Galloway region of the southwest Borders, with some from Kirkcudbrightshire (PANB, 1993).

24 The so-called "Scotch Settlement" in Westmorland County, further to the south, had also attracted Scottish-born families from Prince Edward Island.

25 McDowall, William, *History of the Burgh of Dumfries*, (Dumfries: Wakefield E.P. Publ. Ltd.,1972) p.D48 (from a supplementary chapter by Alfred Truckell).

26 Macleod, Innes Fraser, *Shipping in Dumfries and Galloway in 1820,* Scottish local history texts no. 1 (Kirkcudbright: I. F. MacLeod, 1973) pp. 4–14.

27 The *Augusta* and *Elizabeth,* which were also owned by Thomson, appear only to have had a New Brunswick passenger trade. The *Augusta*'s age and *Lloyd's Register* classification are unknown. The *Elizabeth* was built in 1816 and its *Lloyd's* classification is also unknown.

28 Rayburn, *Geographical Names of Prince Edward Island,* pp. 25, 91; *Dumfries and Galloway Courier,* 21 Feb. 1842.

CHAPTER VI — LATER ARRIVALS FROM SKYE

1 Extract from *Prince Edward Island Register and Gazette,* 2 June, 1829 in MacQueen, *Skye Pioneers and the Island,* pp. 96–7.

2 The *Gazette*'s reference to 84 emigrants was misleading. They were in fact referring to 84 heads of households. Each family who settled in Uigg could purchase between 50 to 100 acres of land. Details of the founding of Uigg are to be found in MacQueen, *Ibid,* pp. 72–73, 92–100.

3 *Inverness Journal,* 30 Jan. 1829.

4 There were Scottish settlers at lot 50 from the 1780s. A few Loyalists settled along

the upper reaches of Orwell Bay in 1784–85. See Clark, *Three Centuries and the Island,* pp. 57–58; also see MacQueen, *Ibid,* pp. 93–9.

5 Kelp is a seaweed common to the area; its ashes were used in glass-making and soap manufacture. Kelp prices were high as it was used as a war-time substitute for imported Spanish material. Prices fell from 1815 and production declined drastically from the mid-1820s. Gray, Malcolm, *The Highland Economy 1750–1850* (Edinburgh: Oliver & Boyd, 1957) pp. 126–51.

6 Emigrant arrivals at this time are difficult to quantify since passenger head-counts are incomplete and in many cases Island arrivals have been subsumed within totals which refer to both the Island as well as Cape Breton.

7 There were widespread clearances on Skye from the mid-1820s as well as in the following decades. Richards, Eric, *A History of the Highland Clearances: Emigration, Protest, Reasons* (London: Croom Helm, 1985) p. 222; Gray, *Highland Economy,* p. 97.

8 *Inverness Journal,* 13 May 1831.

9 *Reports from the Select Committee appointed to inquire into the expediency of encouraging emigration from the United Kingdom,* 1826, IV, Abstract of Petitions.

10 In 1848, about 70 % of Belfast's population (lots 57 and 58) was Church of Scotland; *Prince Edward Island Census, 1848.*

11 MacQueen, *Hebridean Pioneers,* pp. 73–4, 95.

12 PEI Gen Soc. *Survey,* pp. 19–20.

13 Devine, *The Great Highland Famine, Hunger,* pp. 323–6.

14 The scheme, in operation at the time throughout the Highlands, worked on the basis that each Committee paid a contribution of around 10s. per head to each emigrant provided this sum was matched by the proprietor. In all, Lord Macdonald spent £705 on behalf of his Skye tenants and £439 on behalf of his North Uist tenants. The Edinburgh and Glasgow Relief Committees each paid £352 towards the Skye tenants, while the sum of around £200 was paid by each Committee towards Lord MacDonald's North Uist tenants. *SRO GD 221/4434/1.*

15 *Report from the Select Committee appointed to enquire into the condition of the Population of the Highlands and Islands of Scotland, and into the practicability of affording the People relief by means of Emigration,* 1841, VI, A 192. It was estimated that the cost of a steerage passage from the Western Highlands to Prince Edward Island was £4.1s., the sum including transport and food.

16 For example Levitt and Smout concentrate on landlord compulsion in explaining the emigration surges from Skye during the period from 1839 to 1842. Levitt, Ian and Christopher Smout, *The State of the Scottish Working Class in 1843: a statistical and spatial enquiry based on data from the poor law commission report of 1844* (Edinburgh: Scottish Academic Press, 1979) p. 239.

17 Orlo and Fraser, "Elusive Immigrants," *Island Magazine,* No. 18 (1985) p. 34.

18 *Ibid.*

19 PEI Gen, Soc., *Survey,* shows that Skye emigrants arrived at lot 64 from 1829 and at lot 67 from 1830.

20 *Ibid.* The earliest known arrival at Dundas from Skye was in 1826.

21 Some Skye settlers, who emigrated in the 1830s and 1840s, also went to Cape Breton and Upper Canada.

22 *Emigration Select Committee, 1841* A 2, A 189.

23 Freeman, J. D. (ed.) *Samuel Johnson, A Journey to the Western Isles of Scotland* (Oxford, 1985) pp. 48,49,54,69,79–82.

CHAPTER VII — LEAKY TUBS OR FIRST CLASS SHIPS?

1 Extract of letter written by Walter Johnstone in Warburton, *History of Prince Edward Island,* pp. 350–51.
2 *Dumfries Weekly Journal,* 15 Feb. 1820.
3 *Ibid,* 1 Aug. 1820.
4 A full listing of the known ships which took emigrants from Scotland to the Island (1770 to 1850) is provided in Appendix ii.
5 From the time she was built in 1816 until 1821, the *Louisa* regularly carried emigrants from Aberdeen to Halifax. She usually sailed under the same Captain, James Oswald. The *Heroine* took emigrants to Quebec from Aberdeen fairly regularly from 1840 to 1847, usually under the same Captain, Duncan Walker.
6 The registered tonnage of the *Clarendon* was 416 tons, but the *Washington*'s tonnage is not known. Tonnage was a calculated figure which did not necessarily provide an indication of the vessel's capacity to carry a cargo. It was a standard measure used to determine the customs due payable upon registration and navigation fees. Before 1836 the formula was based on only breadth and length but after 1836 it incorporated the vessel's depth as well.
7 *Lloyd's Register* is available as a regular series from 1775 apart from the years 1785, 1788 and 1817.
8 There is some doubt as to whether the *Lovelly Nelly,* listed in the *Lloyd's Register* giving William Sherwin as Captain, is the same *Lovelly Nelly* which took emigrants to the Island in 1774–75 with William Sheridan as Captain. However, given the strong similarity in the names, it is likely that both sources refer to the same ship. The *Register* classified the *Lovelly Nelly* as "I-2," signifying that the hull was in poor condition and that the ship's equipment was of poor quality.
9 Still in use today and run by a Classification Society with a world-wide network of offices and administrative staff, the *Lloyd's Register* continues to provide standard classifications of quality for ship building and maintenance. Blake, George, *Lloyd's Register of Shipping 1760–1960* (London, 1960) pp. 1–7, 26.
10 The number of years that a ship could hold the highest code varied according to where it was built. In time, rivalries developed between shipowners and underwriters and this led to the publication of two Registers between 1800 and 1833— the Shipowners Register (Red Book) and the Underwriters Register (Green Book). Their coverage was similar but not identical. By 1834, with bankruptcies facing both sides, the two Registers joined forces to become the *Lloyd's Register of British and Foreign Shipping.*
11 Emigrant ships which arrived at Prince Edward Island from Scotland were not unique in being of a consistently good quality. This was the general trend for ships which sailed from Scotland to British America with emigrants.
12 No codes could be found for the eight ships which sailed before 1790 largely because of gaps in the *Register.* A ship is not usually distinguishable from others by its name only. To locate a ship's code from the *Register* it is usually necessary to have obtained the tonnage and/or captain's name from other sources. Such

data is not universally available and is highly problematic to locate. Ship tonnage and the master's name can be found readily in the Scottish Customs records (SRO E 504 series), for some years up to 1830, but there are major gaps in the period from 1797–1805 and 1807–1810.

13 Of course, some ships may not have been offered for inspection in the first place. There may have been shippers who stayed clear of the Lloyd's classification system and simply relied on personal contacts to find business. In such cases we would suspect the quality of the shipping on offer. However it is unlikely that many shipowners would have declined to use the Lloyd's system since their ability to attract cargoes would have been severely curtailed.

14 A— first class condition and within a prescribed age limit at the time of sailing; AE (from 1835)—"the second description of the first class," fit, no defects but over a prescribed age limit; E (before 1835)—second class, perfect repair, no defects; E (from 1835)—second class, unfit for carrying dry cargoes but safe for long distance sea voyages; I—third class, only suitable for short voyages (ie. not out of Europe; O (before 1835)—fourth class, out of repair, not safe or sea-worthy. These letters were followed by the number 1 or 2 which signified the condition of the vessel's equipment (anchors, cables and stores). Where satisfactory, the number 1 was used, and where not, 2 was used.

15 *Dumfries and Galloway Courier* 12 Feb. 1822. The *Nancy*'s registered tonnage was 208 tons. "Tons burden" indicates the weight of the ship plus the cargo she could carry.

16 PP 1835(519)XIX. Evidence of Mr Bliss, a shipowner to the *Select Committee on Timber Duties* A 2310 –11.

17 In the early periods of emigration, all agents were depicted as opportunistic money-grubbers who performed no useful function, yet got large sums of money out of vulnerable and misguided emigrants. Occasionally, some agents did deliberately mislead and exploit emigrants but these were isolated cases and such people did no repeat business.

18 Nearly sixty per cent of the 12,000 or so emigrants he acted for, between 1820 and 1832, had gone to Cape Breton. PRO CO 217/154 p. 877, CO 384/67 pp. 235–36: Letters from Archibald MacNiven, 5 April 1832, 19 Jan. 1841.

19 SRO RH 4/188/1, 2: *Prize Essays and Transactions of the Highland Society of Scotland (1799–1834)* Vol. III, pp. 441–4, 475–92, 531–35.

20 Macdonagh, *The Passenger Acts*, pp. 80–9, 148–51, 216–9, 237–45, 337–49 . Harper, *Emigration from North-East Scotland*, pp. 49,105–6; Cowan, *British Emigration,* pp. 152–3 and 168.

21 *Dumfries Weekly Journal*, 15 April 1817.

22 The *General Goldie* was an "A1" sloop and the *North Star* an "E1" schooner.

23 PRO CO 42/170 p. 362.

24 Shipwrecks were an infrequent occurrence and the available evidence shows only very few instances of cholera outbreaks on ships with Scottish passengers.

25 Many scholars and writers have dwelt solely on horrific imagery, having made no independent assessment of the available evidence themselves. Thus we are given preconceptions and not facts. For example, A. R. M. Lower pronounced: "Until about 1835, say, they [emigrants] were probably worse than in the slave trade.

Every slave thrown overboard meant so much money lost; every emigrant less decreased the ship's liability to have to feed him, and more room for those that were left"…"It is impossible to exaggerate the horrors of the emigrant trade." See Lower, Arthur R. M., Great *Britain's Woodyard: British America and the timber trade 1763–1867* (Montreal, 1973) p. 242.

26 Laxton, Edward, *The Famine Ships, The Irish Exodus to America* (New York, 1996).

CHAPTER VIII — HE THINKS HIMSELF ALREADY A PRINCE

1 Anonymous letter writer, *Inverness Journal,* 28 Dec. 1810.
2 Letter, Thomas Wilson, in Charlottetown to his brother in Fife, 9 July 1818: NLS Acc 6981. Modern spelling has been used in the transcription of this letter.
3 Reprinted in the *Aberdeen Journal,* 10 Jan. 1774.

BIBLIOGRAPHY

PRIMARY SOURCES (MANUSCRIPTS)

HIGHLAND COUNCIL ARCHIVES
FAM/INV/25/1 Photocopy of letter from John MacDonald of Glenaladale, 1772.

NATIONAL LIBRARY OF SCOTLAND (NLS)
Adv. MS.73.2.13 Royal Highland and Agricultural Society of Scotland Papers, Letter to Col. MacDonald, 22 Oct., 1791.

MS 9646 *"On Emigration from the Scottish Highlands and Islands attributed to Edward S. Fraser of Inverness-shire"* (1801–4).

MS 11976 Minto Papers, Journal, 1808 concerning emigration from the district to P.E.I..

PUBLIC ARCHIVES OF NOVA SCOTIA (PANS)
MS File Passenger Lists for the *Jane* and *Lucy*, 1790.

PUBLIC ARCHIVES AND RECORDS OFFICE OF PRINCE EDWARD ISLAND (PAPEI)
Abstract of the Census of the Population and other Statistical Returns of Prince Edward Island in the year of 1848.

Acc 2779/1, Chartering of *John and Elizabeth,* 1775.

MSS 2702 Passenger Lists, *Elizabeth and Anne, Spencer* of Newcastle, *Humphreys* of London and *Isle of Skye* of Aberdeen, 1806.

MSS 2704/4 "Early British Emigration to the Maritimes. List of vessels carrying Scottish emigrants to the Maritimes" compiled by Mary Brehaut (1960).

PEI No. 3846 "The Scottish Catholic Church and Prince Edward Island 1770–1810" by J.M. Bumsted pp. 18–33.

RG9 #9 Collector of Customs, 1790–1847.

PUBLIC ARCHIVES OF NEW BRUNSWICK (PANB)
New Brunswick Census, 1861: Kent County.

New Brunswick Census, 1851: Northumberland County.

New Brunswick Census 1851: Restigouche County.

PUBLIC RECORD OFFICE (PRO)
COLONIAL OFFICE PAPERS
CO 42 Correspondence, Canada, 1816.
CO 217/154 Nova Scotia, Original Letters from Scottish shipping agents concerning the Nova Scotia tax, 1832.
CO 226/23 199–208 Prince Edward Island Correspondence, Passenger list, the *Clarendon*, 1808.
CO 226/36 19 Prince Edward Island Correspondence, *Curlew* and *Jane,* 1818.
CO 226/63 31–2 Prince Edward Island Correspondence, Census and Statistical Return of Prince Edward Island, 1841.CO 384/3; 384/67 Emigration, Original Correspondence concerning North American Settlers, 1818, 1841.
TREASURY REGISTERS
T 47/12 Passenger Lists *Lovelly Nelly*, 1774–75.

SCOTTISH CATHOLIC ARCHIVES, EDINBURGH (SCA)
Blairs Letters 3/269/3 Letter to Bishop John MacDonald, 1774.
Oban Papers Passenger Lists, *Jane* and *Lucy,* 1790.

SCOTTISH RECORD OFFICE (SRO)
CS 96 Court of Session Productions.
E504 Customs Records, Collectors Quarterly Accounts, 1776–1830.
GD 51/15/50, 58 Melville Castle Papers.
GD 221/4433/1, 221/4434/1 Lord MacDonald Papers.
RH 4/188/1, 2 Prize essays and Transactions of the Highland Society of Scotland, Vol. iii, 1802–03.
SC 54/2/106 Sheriff Courts, Argyll.

PRIMARY SOURCES (PRINTED)

Brown, Robert, *Strictures and remarks on the Earl of Selkirk's observations on the present state of the Highlands* (Edinburgh, 1806).
Colonial Records of North Carolina, ed. William L. Saunders (Raleigh, 1886–90).
Douglas, Thomas, fifth Earl of Selkirk, *Observations on the Present State of the Highlands of Scotland, with a view of the causes and probable consequences of emigration,* (Edinburgh, 1806).
Glasgow Colonial Society, *First and Seventh Annual Reports of the Glasgow Colonial Society for promoting the religious interests of Scottish settlers in British North America* (Glasgow, 1826, 1833).
Lloyd's Shipping Register 1775–1850.
Meacham & Co., J H, 1880: *Illustrated Historical Atlas of the Province of Prince Edward Island.*
Parliamentary Papers, Emigration Returns for British North America, 1830–1840.
Report from the Select Committee on Timber Duties, 1835, XIX.
Reports from the Select Committee appointed to inquire into the expediency of encouraging emigration from the United Kingdom, 1826, IV; 1826–27, V.
Report from the Select Committee appointed to enquire into the condition of the Popu-

lation of the Highlands and Islands of Scotland, and into the practicability of affording the People relief by means of Emigration, 1841, VI.

Sinclair, Sir John, *First Statistical Account of Scotland,* 21 vols. (Edinburgh, 1791–99).

Telford, Thomas, *A Survey and Report of the Coasts and Central Highlands of Scotland* (London, 1803).

NEWSPAPERS

Aberdeen Herald
Dumfries and Galloway Courier and Herald Dumfries Weekly Journal
Glasgow Courier
Glasgow Herald
Greenock Advertiser
Inverness Courier
Inverness Journal
Prince Edward Island Gazette
Prince Edward Island Register
Prince Edward Island Royal Gazette
Quebec Gazette
Quebec Mercury
Scots Magazine

SECONDARY SOURCES

Adams, Ian and Somerville, Meredyth, *Cargoes of Despair and Hope: Scottish emigration to North America 1603–1803* (Edinburgh: John Donald, 1993).

Baines, Dudley, *Emigration from Europe 1815–1930,* (Basingstoke: Macmillan, 1991).

Bigwood, Frank, "Two Lists of Intending Passengers to the New World, 1770 and 1771", *SG,* vol. xliii (1996) pp. 17–22.

Blake, George, *Lloyd's Register of Shipping 1760–1960* (London, 1960).

Bolger, F. W. P. (ed.) *Canada's Smallest Province: A History of Prince Edward Island,* (Halifax: Nimbus, 1991).

Bumsted, J.M., 'Highland Emigration to the Island of St. John and the Scottish Catholic Church', *Dalhousie Review,* vol. 58 (1978) pp. 511–27.

Bumsted, J. M., *Land Settlement and Politics in Eighteenth Century Prince Edward Island,* (Kingston: McGill Queens, 1987).

Bumsted, J.M., 'Lord Selkirk of PEI', *The Island Magazine,* No. 5 (1978) pp. 3–8.

Bumsted, J. M., *The People's Clearance: Highland emigration to British North America 1770 –1815* (Edinburgh: Edinburgh University Press, 1982).

Bumsted, J. M., *The Scottish Catholic Church and Prince Edward Island 1770–1810* (*PAPEI* no. 3846).

Bumsted, J.M. 'Settlement by Chance: Lord Selkirk and Prince Edward Island', *Canadian Historical Review,* vol. lix (1978) pp. 170–88.

Cameron, Viola Root, *Emigrants from Scotland to America 1774–1775* (Baltimore: Genealogical Publishing Co., 1965)

Campbell, D.F. and R.A. MacLean, *Beyond the Atlantic Roar: A Study of the Nova Scotia Scots* (Toronto: McClelland and Stewart, 1974)

Clark, Andrew, Hill, *Three Centuries and the Island: A historical geography of settle-ment and agriculture in Prince Edward Island, Canada* (Toronto: University of Toronto Press ,1959)

Clark, Andrew H., 'Old World Origins and Religious Adherence in Nova Scotia', *Geographical Review,* vol. l (1960) pp. 317–44.

Cowan, Helen, *British Emigration to British North America; the first hundred years,* (Toronto: University of Toronto Press, 1961)

Davis, Ralph, *The Industrial Revolution and British Overseas Trade,* (Leicester: Leices-ter University Press, 1979). Devine, T.M., *The Great Highland Famine, Hunger, Emigration and the Scottish Highlands in the Nineteenth Century* (Edinburgh: John Donald, 1988).

Dictionary of Canadian Biography, vols. IV–IX (Toronto, 1979–85).

Freeman, J. D. (ed.) *Samuel Johnson, A Journey to the Western Isles of Scotland* (Oxford, 1985).

Ganong, W. F.,"*Monograph of origins of settlements in the province of New Brunswick*" in Transactions of the Royal Society of Canada, second series (10) sections 1–2 (1904) pp. 1–185.

Graham, Ian, Charles, Cargill, *Colonists from Scotland: emigration to North America 1707–83* (New York: Cornell University Press, 1956).

Gray, Malcolm, *The Highland Economy 1750–1850* (Edinburgh: Oliver & Boyd, 1957).

Greenhill, Basil and Anne Giffard, *Westcountrymen in Prince Edward's Isle,* (Toron-to: University of Toronto Press, 1967).

Harper, Marjory, *Emigration from North-East Scotland* Vol. 1, *Willing Exiles* (Aberdeen: Aberdeen University Press, 1988)

Harvey, Daniel Cobb (ed.), *Journeys to the Island of Saint John or Prince Edward Island 1775–1832* (Toronto: MacMillan Co. of Canada, 1955).

Johnston, H. J. M., *British emigration policy 1815–1830: Shovelling out paupers* (Oxford: Clarendon Press, 1972).

Lawson, Rev. James, "Early Scottish Settlement on Prince Edward Island: The Prince-town Pioneers, 1769–1771", *SG,* vol. xli (1994) pp. 112–30.

Lawson, Rev. James, "Passengers on the *Alexander,* Arisaig to St. John's Island, April–June 1772", *SG,* vol. xxxix (1992) pp. 127–43.

Lawson, Rev. James, "*Lucy, Jane* and the 'Bishop', A study in extant Passenger Lists", *SG,* vol. xlii (1995) pp. 1–13.

Levitt, Ian and Christopher Smout, *The State of the Scottish Working Class in 1843: a statistical and spatial enquiry based on data from the poor law commission report of 1844* (Edinburgh: Scottish Academic Press, 1979).

Lower, Arthur R. M., Great *Britain's Woodyard: British America and the Timber Trade 1763–1867* (Montreal: McGill Queen, 1973).

Macdonagh, Oliver, *A pattern of government growth 1800–1860; the Passenger Acts and their enforcement* (London: MacGibbon and Kee, 1961).

MacDonald, Colin S., "Early Highland Emigration to Nova Scotia and Prince Edward Island from 1770 to 1853", *Nova Scotia Historical Society (Collections),* vol. xxiii (1936) pp. 41–48.

MacEwan, Andrew, B. W., "The Falmouth Passengers", *The Island Magazine,* vol. 10 (1981) pp. 12–19.

MacKay, Ian, R., "Glenaladale's Settlement in Prince Edward Island", *Scottish Gaelic Studies,* vol. x (1965) pp. 17–20.

MacKenzie, John Munro, *Diary, 1851, John Munro MacKenzie, Chamberlain of the Lews* (Stornoway, Isle of Lewis: Acair, 1994).

Malpeque Historical Society, *Malpeque and Its People 1700–1982* (Malpeque, 1982).

MacLeod, Harold S., *The Macleods of Prince Edward Island* (Montague, P.E.I., 1986).

MacLeod, Innes Fraser, *Shipping in Dumfries and Galloway in 1820,* Scottish local history texts no. 1 (Kirkcudbright: I.F. MacLeod, 1973).

MacNutt, W. S., *The Atlantic Provinces; the emergence of Colonial Society 1712–1857* (London: McClelland and Stewart, 1965).

MacQueen, Malcolm A., *Hebridean Pioneers* (Winnipeg, 1957).

MacQueen, Malcolm, *Skye Pioneers and the Island* (Winnipeg: Stovel Co., 1929).Martell, J.S. *Immigration to and Emigration from Nova Scotia 1815–1838* (Halifax: PANS 1942).

Martin, Chester, *Lord Selkirk's Work in Canada* , Oxford Historical and Literary Studies, vol. 7 (Oxford, 1916).

McDowall, William, *History of the Burgh of Dumfries,* (Dumfries: Wakefield E. P. Publ. Ltd., 1972).

MacLaren, George, *The Pictou Book* (New Glasgow, N.S., 1954).

Meyer, D. Vane, *The Highland Scots of North Carolina* (Durham: University of Carolina Press, 1961).

Moir, John S., *The Church in the British Era, from the British Conquest to Confederation* (Toronto: McGraw-Hill Ryerson, 1972).

Morse, Susan Longley, "Immigration to Nova Scotia 1839–51" (Dalhousie, Nova Scotia, unpublished M.A. 1946).

Nicholson, John et al., *Middle River, Past and Present history of a Cape Breton community 1806–1985* (Cape Breton, 1985).

Orlo, J. and Fraser D., "Those Elusive Immigrants, Parts 1 to 3", *Island Magazine,* No. 16 (1984) pp. 36–44, No. 17 (1985) pp. 32–7, No. 18 (1985) pp. 29–35.

Prince Edward Island Genealogical Society, *From Scotland to Prince Edward Island: Scottish emigrants to Prince Edward Island from death and obituary notices in Prince Edward Island 1835–1910* (n.d.).

Rayburn, Alan, *Geographical Names of Prince Edward Island; Toponymy Study* (Ottawa: Department of Energy, Mines and Resources, 1973).

Richards, Eric, *A History of the Highland Clearances: Emigration, Protest, Reasons* (London: Croom Helm, 1985).

Roberston, Ian Ross, "Highlanders, Irishmen and the Land Question in Nineteenth Century Prince Edward Island" in J.M. Bumsted (ed.), *Interpreting Canada's Past* Vol. 1 (Toronto: Oxford University Press, 1986) pp. 359–73.

The Scottish Catholics in Prince Edward Island 1772–1922, Memorial Volume (Summerside: Journal Publishing Co., 1922)

Straus, Ralph, *Lloyds: A Historical Sketch* (London: Hutchinson & Co., 1937).

Warburton, A. B., *History of Prince Edward Island* (St. John, N.B., 1923).

White, Patrick Cecil Telford, (ed.) *Lord Selkirk's Diary 1803–04; A journal of his travels through British North America and the Northeastern United States* (Toronto: The Champlain Soc., 1958).

Wynn, Graeme, *Timber Colony: an historical geography of early nineteenth century New Brunswick* (Toronto: University of Toronto Press, 1981).

INDEX

Moidart (Inverness-shire), 25, 136
Montgomery, James (Sir), 20, 21, 23, 24, 136, 137, 153, 154
Montgomery, Hugh, 105, 154
Montgomery settlement, 154
Montreal (Quebec), 62, 143
Morar (Inverness-shire), 25, 138
Morayshire, 29, 30, 33, 137, 156
Morrow, John, 154
Mull, Isle of, 22, 40, 55, 58, 64, 81, 101, 102, 140, 143, 159
Mullins, James, 70
Munroe, Donald, 84
Munroe, Mary, 84
Murchison, _____ (Mrs. Alexander), 40
Murchison, Peter, 35
Murray Harbour (lots 63 & 64), 87

Napoleonic Wars, 10, 12–15, 47, 49, 64, 72, 97, 101, 152, 159
Native Peoples, 17
New Abbey (Kirkcudbrightshire), 30, 71
New Annan (lot 19), 71, 77, 78, 160
New Argyle (lots 30 & 65), 8, 55, 64, 160
New Brunswick, 65, 69, 70, 72, 75–77, 102, 135, 139, 140, 144–147, 149, 156, 161
New Brunswick Census, 72
New Brunswick Royal Gazette, 73
New Carlisle (Quebec), 144
Newcastle, 53, 97, 124, 127, 141, 143
Newfoundland, 67, 90, 91, 140
New Glasgow (lot 23), 62, 150
New London (lots 20 & 21), 60
New Perth (lots 51 & 52), 21, 58, 62, 142
New York, 18, 68, 71, 153
Nicolson, Donald, 34
Nicolson, John, 34
Nicolson, John, 34
Nicolson, Mary, 40
Nith, river, 90
North Carolina, 5, 18, 36, 39, 89, 138, 153, 156

North West Highlands, 12
Northumberland Strait, 12, 76, 102
Nova Scotia, 10, 12, 27, 36, 37, 60, 72, 96, 138, 140, 145, 152, 158

Oban, xi, 52–54, 92, 93, 124, 130, 142, 158
Oban Harbour, 93
"Old World Origins and Religious Adherence to Nova Scotia," 11
Orwell Bay (Cove) (lots 50 & 57), 39, 40, 81, 137, 162

PEI Gen. Soc Survey (see Scottish Emigration to Prince Edward Island)
Panmure Island (lot 61), 57
Panting, Jane, 40
Passenger Act (1803), 33, 53, 96–98, 156, 158, 159
Passenger Fares (sea crossings), 105, 106, 159, 162
Passenger List(s); 10, 53, 54, 105
  Clarendon, 130
  Edinburgh, 105, 106
  Elizabeth and Ann, 127
  Humphreys, 119
  Isle of Skye, 122
  Lovelly Nelly (2), 107
  Jane, 112
  Lucy, 114
  Rambler, 115
  Spencer, 124
Peeblesshire, 137
Peenorcronan (Skye), 34
Peingown and Osmigarry (Skye), 34
Peoples Clearance, The, 105, 153
Perthshire, 16, 19–21, 57–59, 62–64, 92, 103, 136, 143, 154, 159
Philadelphia, 75
Pictou (Nova Scotia), 30, 37, 51, 56, 60, 73, 74, 76, 137, 140–142, 143, 145, 146, 148–150, 158
Pictou Harbour, 30
Pinette (lot 58 & 59), 40
Plaster Rock (Nova Scotia), 145

About the Author

Lucille Campey is a Canadian, living in Britain, with over thirty years experience as a researcher and author. It was her father's Scottish roots and love of history which first stimulated her interest in the early exodus of people from Scotland to Canada. She is the great-great-granddaughter of William Thomson, who left Morayshire, on the northeast coast of Scotland, in the early 1800s to begin a new life with his family, first near Digby, then in Antigonish, Nova Scotia. He is described in D. Whidden's History of the Town of Antigonish simply as "William, Pioneer" and is commemorated in the St. James Church and Cemetery at Antigonish.

Lucille's book on Prince Edward Island's Scottish pioneers is the culmination of ten years of research and is based on her doctoral thesis completed at Aberdeen University. She lived in Tain, in Easter Ross, for five of these years and during this time visited many of the major Archives and Reference Libraries throughout Scotland.

A Chemistry graduate of Ottawa University, Lucille worked initally in the fields of science and computing. After marrying her English husband, she moved to the north of England where she became interested in medieval monasteries and acquired a Master of Philosophy degree (on the subject of medieval settlement patterns) from Leeds University. She travels to Toronto regularly to see her brother and has occasional holidays in the eastern Maritimes. She and her husband now live near Salisbury in Wiltshire.